MINOR HINTS

MINOR HINTS

LECTURES DELIVERED

TO

H. H. THE MAHARAJA GAEKWAR, SAYAJI RAO III , G.C.S.I.

RAJA SIR T. MADHAVA RAO, K.C.S.I.

GYAN

Published by

Gyan Publishing House
5, Ansari Road
Daryaganj, New Delhi-110002
Phone: 011-47034999, 9811692060
E-mail: books@gyanbooks.com

Distribution Network
gyanbooks.com
India, USA, Canada, UK, Australia, France

ISBN : 978-81-212-9514-7 (PB)
First Published, 1881

2nd Impression 2023

Printed at: Gyan Press, Delhi.

MINOR HINTS
Author: RAJA SIR T. MADHAVA RAO

LECTURES DELIVERED

TO

H. H. THE MAHARAJA GAEKWAR, SAYAJI RAO III, G.C.S.I.,

BY

RAJA SIR T. MADHAVA RAO, K.C.S.I.

MINOR HINTS.

CONTENTS.

MINOR HINTS

CHAPTER I

SUBSCRIPTIONS

His Highness the Maharaja is sure to receive numerous applications for subscriptions and contributions to various objects and institutions. One applicant will ask for a number of copies being taken of a book which he is about to publish. Another will solicit aid for building a temple, or a ghaut, or a dharamsala. A third will solicit a donation for horse-races. His Highness' liberality will be invoked in favour of schools, hospitals, theatrical performances, horse-shows, fine arts, new industries, and diverse other purposes.

Numerous applications.

(2) It is obvious that all such applications cannot be complied with. Due discrimination will have to be exercised by the Maharaja. Each case will have to be judged on its own merits, but the following considerations may afford some useful guidance.

Judge each on its merits.

(3) It is to be remembered that the money concerned is part of the taxes paid by the people of Baroda, and therefore cannot be arbitrarily or capriciously given away. Grants of such money may be made mainly for objects which directly or indirectly benefit the people of Baroda.

Subscription to benefit the people of Baroda.

(4) Contributions destined to be spent within the limits of Baroda territories are generally to be preferred to those which are to be spent outside those territories.

Prefer local contributions.

(5) Those which benefit the poor are to be preferred to those which benefit the rich.

And those to the poor and to relieve pain.

Those which relieve pain are to be preferred to those which afford pleasure.

(6) The amount of contribution should be moderate so as to necessitate and induce others also to contribute. In other words, our contribution should not be so large as to induce others to say "From Baroda alone much of the required funds have come. We need not therefore give anything ourselves."

Amount to be moderate.

(7) Anything given should be in reference to the usefulness of the object, and not prompted by a mere spirit of vanity or rivalry, or by the pressure of importunity on the part of the applicant.

The object to be useful.

Discourage periodical subscriptions.

(8) It is better to give donations once for all or at sufficient intervals, than to commit the State to continuous monthly subscriptions from which it would be difficult to withdraw when necessary or desirable, owing to altered circumstances.

Examples.

a. **Racing.**

(9) I may here adduce a few instances in elucidation of the foregoing principles.

(*a*) Baroda should not contribute to horse-racing at Bangalore or Bombay—in short, any place outside Baroda. Even at Baroda any expenditure in this direction must be moderate and occasional as our people do not take much interest in racing.

b. **Fine arts.**

(*b*) Baroda should not contribute to fine arts in Europe or America, but it should not be indifferent to the fine arts of India.

c. **Works of utility.**

(*c*) Better to contribute for the construction of a bathing *ghaut* on some river in Baroda territories, than for one on the Godavery, or the Krishna, or the Cauvery.

CHAPTER II

HINTS ON PERSONAL CONDUCT

8th June 1881

By way of some variety, I purpose to offer a few minor hints bearing on personal conduct. They will be offered just as they occur, but may be easily arranged in some order at the end. The hints are for consideration and for such attention as they may be found to deserve. Several may possibly be unnecessary, because they are self-evident, or because they are already known. Yet they are offered with the rest, because it is not easy to distinguish the one from the other.

They are Self-evident.

(1) When things have to be ordered from merchants, shop-keepers, etc., etc., His Highness the Maharaja need not address letters to such persons under his own signature. All business, in short, with such persons should be conducted for His Highness by some of his officials, such as Mr. Raoji Vithal.

No Correspondence with tradesmen.

Private correspondence to be limited.

(2) All sorts of individuals will constantly address His Highness private letters on various subjects. Great care and discrimination will have to be used in sending replies. The needless growth of private correspondence should be prevented. Letters and notes from the Maharaja should be rather rare as a rule. It would not be good that lots of common people should go about saying that they correspond with His Highness and parading his letters and notes. Many things lose their value by becoming too common.

Record to be kept.

(3) Arrangements should be made for keeping copies of all letters or notes sent by the Maharaja. It will be useful in many ways. So communications received by His Highness should be kept regularly by some official. Very small matters sometimes become important, and hence the papers must be available.

Important communications to be previously seen.

(4) In many instances, some official will have to address communications as directed by His Highness. Great care must be taken in order that the official does not go beyond the directions of His Highness, or use language not intended or desired by His Highness. Communications addressed as directed by His Highness, of course, commit His Highness and hence the

care required. As a rule, the drafts of such communications should be previously seen by His Highness and initialled with a view to prevent mistakes.

Use the best Stationery.

(5) Letters and notes from His Highness should be on the most approved paper. The best ink, envelopes, &c., should be used. Everything should be neat so as to befit His Highness' exalted position.

His Highness' visits not to be too common.

(6) The personal visit of the Maharaja is in itself a great honour. Its value should not be diminished by making such visits too common. I refer to occasions of marriage and other ceremonies in private families. What precedents exist, may, of course, be attended to. But care has to be used in going beyond those precedents.

Introduction of strangers by a responsible officer and not a menial.

(7) If any stranger desires to pay a visit to His Highness, he must not do so without somebody to intrcduce him. The general rule should be that he should be properly introduced to His Highness, otherwise, all sorts of objectionable people will obtain admittance, which would not befit His Highness' position and dignity. It might be even unsafe.

It would not suffice that anybody introduces the strangers to the Maharaja. For instance, jasoods, menial servants and such persons are not proper parties to introduce. The introducer must be a person of position and responsibility. He should be held responsible that he does not introduce improper persons to His Highness, such as bad or condemned characters, low persons who are not in the category of gentlemen, unscrupulous adventurers and so forth. The introducer is responsible to fairly satisfy himself of the respectability of the stranger before introducing him to the Maharaja. In this respect the Palace arrangements may well be like those at Government House, Bombay or Calcutta.

The Maharaja to have previous information.

(8) When a stranger is to be introduced to His Highness, His Highness should have some previous information regarding that stranger, so that His Highness may know how to receive and treat him, what to say to him, and so forth.

Promises not to be made hastily.

(9) Many persons will press His Highness with many solicitations. The Maharaja has to be careful not to commit himself to hasty opinions or hasty promises. Generally, it is desirable for the Maharaja to take time to consult and reflect before expressing any decided opinion, or making any definite promise. Great caution has thus to be exercised by those who are in high positions and power.

CHAPTER III

Menials and Intriguers

Wednesday, 22nd June 1881

The Maharaja should avoid familiarity with menial servants. These must be kept at a respectful distance, and must be limited to their respective duties.

Avoid familiarity with menials.

(2) The menial servants must be placed under the control and supervision of some responsible official who should see that they behave properly ; and such official should have some power over these servants, so as to be able to influence them by means of hope and fear.

Official to check them.

(3) The menial servants should be prevented from overhearing the Maharaja's conversations and reporting them abroad. Unless vigilantly looked after, they are generally only too apt to sell news of this kind.

They should not overhear.

(4) They should be prevented from going about to see the Sirdars, Darakdars, &c., and also the officers, sowkars and people generally, and begging for presents and gratuities on one pretence or

Nor be allowed to beg.

another. The Maharaja's servants making money in this way would be quite opposed to the dignity of the Maharaja, while it would put people to inconvenience.

Visitors to be independent of them.

(5) The arrangements in relation to visitors to the Maharaja must be so made, that they may be quite independent of the favour or disfavour of these menial servants.

Menials not to indulge in criticism.

(6) The menial servants must, on no account, be permitted to speak to the Maharaja, or in the presence of the Maharaja about matters which are far above them. For instance, they must not indulge in political discussions, or speak of the merits of Ministers.

Nor to present petitions.

(7) They must not be allowed to introduce strangers to the Maharaja, or to present petitions to the Maharaja on behalf of any stranger, or indeed on behalf of any one.

To be polite.

(8) They must be enjoined to be polite to visitors and others.

Post-mortem examination when necessary.

(9) Whenever any sudden, violent, or suspected death of any servants—indeed of any one—occurs in the Palace, the Maharaja should, by all means, direct a regular *post-mortem* examination, with the view of ascertaining and recording the real cause

of death. This is a very necessary precaution to avert serious scandals or suspicions.

Wages to be cash.

(10) As far as possible, fix the wages or remuneration of the Palace servants in cash. This is most convenient to all concerned. The allowance of "seedhas" (provisions in kind) is always liable to great abuse.

No arbitrary dismissal.

(11) Palace servants are generally in the position of private servants. Yet, it is desirable that they should feel confident of continued employment, so long as they behave well. In other words, as a rule, they should not be arbitrarily or capriciously dismissed; and they should be promoted according to their good behaviour and as opportunities occur.

Liberal salaries to personal servants.

(12) Such menial servants as have much to do personally with the Maharaja should have really liberal salaries and should be so treated as to feel great personal devotion to His Highness. In instances of any specially good behaviour, they may be occasionally rewarded so as to encourage them. The same remarks equally apply to servants personally in service with the Maharanees and the children.

Punishment to be proportionate.

(13) The minor faults of such servants should not be too rigidly noticed or punished. All menial servants have such faults more or less. We must only see that they do not go beyond minor faults.

The Maharaja not to take a personal part.

(14) If any of the Palace servants so misbehave as to call for punishment, even then the Maharaja had better not appear to take a very prominent or active personal part in their punishment. Let that punishment be by the Palace officers, or by the public Magistracy, as the case may be. The object is to avoid, as far as may be possible, His Highness becoming an object of personal hatred.

The hereditary principle of employment is desirable.

(15) Giving effect to the hereditary principle in regard to Palace servants, as far as may be convenient, is rather a desirable thing within certain limits, as it is conducive to greater attachment on the part of the servants. If an old servant dies or becomes disabled from age, sickness, or other cause, better give some employment to his son or brother, and so on. But the hereditary principle is quite objectionable in the public service where special qualifications are required.

Avoid intriguers.

(16) All Palaces are, more or less, infested by intriguers. The Maharaja has to exercise constant vigilance against falling into their snares. As soon as the Maharaja is installed in power—and even before—these intriguers will try their tricks. Therefore, a few hints in this direction may be of use.

(17) Intriguers are generally persons who are very selfish in their motives and who are devoid of, or deficient in, good principles. They are excessively fond of secret representations. They make false or reckless statements. They grossly exaggerate matters. They give a false colouring to circumstances. They endeavour to make themselves agreeable by constant flattery and obsequiousness. By bearing these distinguishing qualities in mind, and by means of close observation, some intriguers may be found out. When the Maharaja is able to discover intriguers by such means, His Highness should refuse to give ear to them. They should be kept at great distance. In short, the less the Maharaja has to do with them, the better will it be for His Highness' interests.

They are selfish and only flatter.

(18) Again, if any person is known to have been an intriguer in past times, he may be generally presumed to be an intriguer at present also, unless there is any clear reason to suppose that the person has undergone a complete reformation. As a general rule, therefore, the Maharaja should keep at a distance such persons as are known to have practised intrigues in past times.

Intriguers of past times to be kept aloof.

(19) Again, if the Maharaja is assured that such and such a person is an intriguer—assured by some of those

Trust faithful advisers.

whom the Maharaja recognizes as his sincere well-wishers and faithful advisers—His Highness will do well to accept such assurance and keep the intriguer at a distance. At any rate, the Maharaja should specially scrutinize the man. Acting on the foregoing hints, the Maharaja will be able to get rid of numbers of intriguers though not of the whole lot.

The qualities of an intriguer and a well-wisher.

(20) On further consideration, it appears to me that what I have thus far stated is not sufficient. To make the matter still more clear, I proceed to give below, in *juxtaposition*, the qualities which mark an intriguer and those which mark a real well-wisher.

INTRIGUER.	REAL WELL-WISHER.
Not a real well-wisher. (*a*) An intriguer is not a real well-wisher but one who simulates a well-wisher	(*a*) A real well-wisher is what he is.
Base. (*b*) In other words, an intriguer is base metal only coated with gold.	(*b*) A real well-wisher is a solid mass of gold.
Bad antecedents. (*c*) An intriguer is generally one whose antecedents show him to be an intriguer.	(*c*) A real well-wisher's antecedents show him to be a blameless man.

Known as such. (*d*) An intriguer is generally known as such by good men.	(*d*) A real well-wisher is generally known as such by good men.
Discontented. (*e*) An intriguer is generally a discontented man and thinks that he has been badly treated and kept down.	(*e*) A real well-wisher has no particular discontent and is satisfied with his lot, like any ordinary man.
Thinks to much of himself. (*f*) An intriguer has generally a very high opinion of his own ability and skill.	(*f*) A real well-wisher estimates himself at his work.
Selfish. (*g*) The principal actuating motive of an intriguer is selfishness.	(*g*) The principal actuating motive of a real well-wisher is not selfishness.
Hope of large benefit. (*h*) An intriguer works with the object of obtaining some large benefit for himself—for instance, he wants high employment in the public service, etc.	(*h*) A real well-wisher aims at the good of the Maharaja and of the people.
No secret of his designs. (*i*) An intriguer will generally make representations which directly or indirectly points to the desirableneess of his being benefitted in the way he desires.	(*i*) A real well-wisher will not confine himself to topics in which his personal interest is involved but will speak more at large.

Attacks men.

(*j*) An intriguer will generally speak more against men than against measures.

(*j*) A real well-wisher will speak more against measures than against men.

Particularly those in his way.

(*k*) An intriguer will generally speak most against those men who stand in the way of his obtaining the benefit he desires.

(*k*) A real well-wisher will speak generally of al men.

Gives them no credit.

(*l*) An intriguer will generally give no credit whatever to those men, but will condemn them in every way.

(*l*) A real well-wisher will give credit where due. He will be more discriminating.

Speak vaguely

(*m*) Against those men, the intriguer will speak in general and very vague terms. For example, he will say that those men are bad; that they are unfaithful; that they are doing mischief; that they are selfish; that they wish to get the favour of the British Government at the expense of the Native State, and so forth.

(*m*) A real well-wisher will be more specific. If he finds fault, he will exactly say on what account.

Draws adverse inferences.

(*n*) An intriguer will draw adverse inferences from any facts indiscriminately. For instance, if the revenues have increased, he will say that the people suffer from increased exactions. If the revenues have diminished, he will say that the State has suffered loss owing to mismanagement. If the expenditure has increased, he will say that it is the effect of extravagance and carelessness. If the expenditure has diminished, he will say that it is the effect of stinginess and of unfair reductions.

(*n*) A real well-wisher will give more impartial opinions. He will distinguish between legitimate and illegitimate causes of variation.

Misrepresents facts.

(*o*) An intriguer has little or no scruples. He will for his own selfish ends, misrepresent or distort facts and circumstances so as to tell against those who are opposed to his own interests.

(*o*) A real well-wisher will scrupulously state facts as they are.

Even tells lies.

(*p*) An intriguer will even tell downright falsehoods to serve his own purpose, where the falsehood is not easily discoverable.

(*p*) A real well-wisher will never tell falsehoods. He will be perfectly truthful. Though he may criticise measures he will generally give credit for good motives and

For instance, he will impute all sorts of bad motives or intentions to his opponents.

Calls errors acts of mischief.

(*q*) An intriguer will be most eager to lay hold of mere errors or slips, such as the best of men must, more or less, commit and will construe such errors into deliberate acts of mischief on the part of his opponents.

Works secretly.

(*r*) An intriguer is generally fond of darkness. He would actually prefer to make his visits during night. He always wishes to meet you secretly. He is full of mysterious whispers, hints and predictions. He makes it appear that what he discloses to you is only a very small part of what he knows of the misdoings of his opponents. He would frequently request you not to divulge what he says to you and would thus prevent you from obtaining the means of testing the truth of his allegations.

good intentions.

(*q*) A real well-wisher will act more generously. He will recognize the fact that the best men are not infallible. He will recognize the great difference between mere error and a deliberate act.

(*r*) A real well-wisher behaves differently from all this.

Promotes bad feelings.

(*s*) An intriguer, when he has not much to say on public grounds, is extremely fond of trying to bring about bad feelings between you and his opponents on private or trivial grounds. For instance, he would say that such an officer looks upon you with contempt; that that officer, the other day, said so and so about you—and so forth. Ask the intriguer where the officer spoke so? The reply would be that the words were spoken at home by the officer to one of his friends. Query—Would that friend tell me all about it if I refer to him? Answer—Would he betray his friend? Question—How did you, then, come to know of it? Answer—A certain servant of that officer overheard the contemptuous words. Question—Would that servant say all about it to me if called before me? Answer—How would the servant betray his master? Question—Let me

(*s*) A real well-wisher would not stoop to such proceedings. He would rather advise the Maharaja not to listen for a moment to such tales—nor to listen to what this man or that man said in private, even if true, for an officer's conduct is to be judged by his official acts.

then ask you again, how did you come to know of it? Answer—As you press me I must reveal the truth. The servant of that officer and my servant are friends. The former gave the information to the latter. My servant told me all about it. Question—Would your servant repeat it to me? Answer—I am not sure but he may, if assured of protection. Therefore, perhaps, the simple Maharaja actually sends for that servant of the intriguer and questions him, after assuring him of protection and holding out some prospects of reward. And the servant repeats what he had been tutored by the intriguer himself to say! The Maharaja, ignorant of the rules of evidence, considers the matter proved! The intriguer then submits a few general remarks. He says it was a fortunate thing that the matter was proved to His Highness in this instance. But in many instances, such matters cannot be proved.

If so severely cross-examined by His Highness and put to proof it would be very hard, and it would be better hereafter not to give any information. The Maharaja is thus induced to say "Never mind, I am now satisfied. You may go on giving me information without any fear." Under some such assurance, dose after dose of poison is administered, until the officer concerned is ruined in His Highness' estimation.

He would do anything to please the Maharaja.

(*t*) Another characteristic of an intriguer is that he would do anything to please the Maharaja. He would never express any opinion different from His Highness'. On the contrary, anything His Highness says, however trivial, he would applaud in terms of admiration except as regards matters relative to the opponents against whom his intrigues are directed. He would assiduously cultivate the friendship of the Maharaja's principal friends

(*t*) A real well-wisher would avoid flattery and adulation. He would frankly express his own opinion, whether it happens to coincide with yours or not. He would behave with self-respect. He would be polite to your principal friends and relations, but would not go out of his way to court their favour in the manner as the intriguer would do.

and relations by various means, as for instance, by lending money, making acceptable presents, promising to do all sorts of service for them when he gets into power, and so forth.

The Maharaja to study character.

(21) Your Highness will do well to study thoroughly the foregoing characteristics. I have given you the result of long and careful observations. The foregoing furnish to you pretty good means, wherewith you may be largely able to judge for yourself to say that such a person is an intriguer and not a real well-wisher—to say that this is brass and not gold. Of course, you will have to apply the tests patiently and attentively. The motives, the aims, the allegations, and the deportment of the given individual will have to be very carefully observed, with reference to the criteria. I have categorically stated. The Maharaja has frequent occasions to do this, for he has frequent occasions to judge of men. The process may appear somewhat laborious first. But repeated exercise will make it easy till you are able to judge almost with the rapidity of natural instinct.

General allegations of fact of no practical value.

(22) What an intriguer may say may be regarded in another aspect. Whatever he says must consist of allegations of fact and of opinion. Now,

opinions from such a source are entitled to little or no weight. If the Maharaja seeks opinions, he may go to the reliable, recognized and responsible source. Allegations of fact remain. These are either vague and general or clear and specific. Vague and general allegations of fact are of little or no practical use. They may be generally rejected. Thus there remain only clear and specific allegations of facts. If these are of sufficient importance, and if they appear probable, or are supported by *prima facie* evidence, the Maharaja may take some notice of them.

An example.

(23) To make this further clear, let us take an example. Suppose an intriguer says to the Maharaja, "Mr. A. is a very bad judge. He takes bribes. In such a case, the other day, he took a bribe of 1,000 Rupees from such a person." Here, the first sentence merely expresses an opinion entitled to little or no weight. The second sentence contains a vague and general allegation of fact of little or no practical use. It is only the third sentence which contains a clear and specific allegation of fact. If the person alleging is prepared to give evidence or to point to evidence, then the Maharaja may direct his Ministerto make such enquiry as may be desirable, and to report the particulars of the enquiry and the result thereof.

Only specific allegations of fact to be considered.

(24) The example I have above given is an extremely simple one, intended simply to make my meaning clear. But allegations of the kind are, generally, long and complex. They should all be sifted carefully with reference to the foregoing suggestions; and we should find out what the several clear and specific and important allegations of fact are, which alone have to be considered. In the course of my experience, I have found many an intriguer unable to stand such a sifting process.

Beware of unscrupulous persons.

(25) The Maharaja must know and constantly apply this sifting process. Otherwise, he will be apt to be carried away by long and wordy statements—to be deceived by designing and unscrupulous persons.

CHAPTER IV

ANGER

Wednesday, 29*th June* 1881

The best of us are, at times, liable to anger. And a Maharaja's position is such that his temper and patience will be daily exposed to trial. Again, the Maharaja being the highest personage in the State, there are few persons who can exercise a check on him in this respect. Lastly, it is to be remembered that any harm or mischief arising from anger would be much greater in the instance of the Maharaja, than in that of a private individual.

The Maharaja's temper daily exposed to trial.

(2) These circumstances show how the Maharaja has need to be specially careful against the evils of anger. His Highness should, therefore, use his best endeavours to avoid anger altogether. Repeated efforts will establish the habit of taking things calmly and coolly.

Take things coolly.

(3) When, however, in spite of every effort to the contrary, the Maharaja finds that anger has taken possession of him, then His Highness will do well to remember

Anger is temporary madness.

the following considerations. Anger is an excitement of the mind which is, in many respects, like temporary madness. In that state of excitement, the mind takes one particular direction in a violent manner, and is blind to those facts and reasons which require to be taken into account in order to form a sound judgment. In short, during anger, the most necessary and the most valuable faculty of judgment is in a state of paralysis.

When angry, refrain from acting or speaking.

(4) In such a state of mind the safest course to pursue is to altogether refrain from acting or even speaking in regard to the matter which has excited that state of mind. Better altogether drop the matter for the time, and turn the mind to something else—going to sleep will be a capital thing, for, it has such an excellent pacifying effect, or His Highness may take a long ride or drive; or His Highness may devote himself to reading some interesting book.

Draw the mind away and avoid unpleasantness.

(5) I would strongly recommend that the mind be thus drawn away from the subject matter of the mental disturbance. If possible, better not return to that subject matter for a week or ten days. By following this somewhat simple advice, the Maharaja will save himself from many wrong acts and offensive expressions, which, if

indulged in, might involve him in political embarrassment, or might entail upon him the loss of friends and well-wishers, or might inflict serious discouragement upon his faithful servants and dependents.

How to get Another's Opinion

Avoid expressing your own.

(1) If the Maharaja desires to invite any person's opinion, the Maharaja had better refrain from expressing his own opinion at the outset. His Highness' own opinion had better not be even indicated or implied. Even should the person spoken to ask for His Highness' opinion, better avoid expressing it, if possible.

Two reasons (*a*) the other person may not express a different opinion.

(2) There are two main reasons for this suggestion: (*a*) If His Highness' opinion be expressed at the outset, the person addressed might hesitate to express a contrary or different opinion. At least he might feel a certain degree of restraint. But the object is to get the person's opinion as freely expressed as possible. (*b*) Again, any opinion prematurely formed by the Maharaja—formed before knowing the opinions of other persons—might be incorrect; and it is not desirable that His Highness should needlessly run the risk of expressing crude and incorrect opinions which would have to be given up upon due deliberation and consultation.

(*b*) The Maharaja's opinion may be incorrect.

CHAPTER V

FIRMNESS

20th July 1881

Firmness is a virtue which is desirable in all persons, and exceedingly desirable in those whom Providence has made rulers. If a Maharaja is wanting in firmness, it becomes very difficult to carry on public business. He has one opinion at one time and a different opinion at another. He has one purpose at one time, and a different purpose at another. He orders one thing now and orders a different thing shortly afterwards.

A Maharaja must be firm.

(2) Genuine firmness is the result of careful study of facts, careful reasoning, and correct conclusions. It is the consciousness of having carefully studied the facts, of having carefully reasoned and of having correctly judged,—it is the consciousness of having properly performed these processes, that makes the mind firm. A Maharaja who has himself performed these processes will be quite right to feel and manifest firmness.

Careful reasoning makes one firm.

(3) It would, however, be impossible for the Maharaja to himself perform these processes in the thousand instances in which he has to act. Is he then to be fickle in all those instances? No. If he were to be unsteady in all those instances, the conduct of public business would suffer very much.

Do not be unsteady.

(4) In those instances, then, the Maharaja should trust his trustworthy and responsible counsellors who have themselves performed the processes above mentioned. He should generally, in such instances, accept the opinions and advice given by such counsellors, and show firmness of mind in acting upon such opinions and advice. What I have just mentioned is a very important principle which the Maharaja should thoroughly understand. If he does not understand and act upon that principle, he will be constantly placed in painfully embarrassing positions in daily life. Remember, it is only in a few—very few—instances, that he can himself collect facts, reason on them, and form a correct judgment. In the great majority of instances in which he cannot perform these processes, what is he to do? Is he to be fickle? Then, the public business will materially suffer. Is he to form an arbitrary conclusion and stick to it? Then the public business will suffer still more. It is a bad dilemma.

Trust responsible counsellors.

(5) History shows many examples of public affairs suffering in the manner just stated, because of the ruler concerned not understanding and acting on the principle under advertence. It will be found that those rulers who have been remarkable for the virtue of firmness have eminently known the principle, how to select worthy and faithful counsellors, to accept the carefully formed opinion and advice of such counsellors, and to exercise the virtue of firmness as founded thereon.

Firm rulers know how to select their men.

(6) From what I have already stated, it must be evident that firmness in a virtue when it is exercised in relation to right conclusions only. It is then a very valuable virtue in rulers. But the moment it comes to be exercised in relation to wrong conclusions, the quality ceases to be a virtue. It becomes a mischievous vice. It becomes simple obstinacy.

Obstinacy.

(7) The vital difference between the virtue of firmness and the vice of obstinacy arises from the conclusions in the first place being right and the conclusion in the second case being wrong. Every ruler has, therefore, need to make sure that he is firm and that he is not obstinate by making sure that his conclusion is right and that it is not wrong. A firm Maharaja will do much good. An obstinate Maharaja will do much harm.

Difference between firmness and obstinacy.

Obstinacy not to be mistaken for firmness.

(8) This difference between the virtue of firmness and the vice of obstinacy must be constantly remembered, lest obstinacy be mistaken for firmness. The virtue and the vice have much in common, and therefore a weak-minded ruler is only too apt to mistake the latter for the former. But a strong-minded ruler, with the advantage of education, and with the further advantage of previous warning, will remember the essential difference between the virtue and the vice, and make sure that he has the virtue and not the vice.

A wise ruler should change his view, if wrong.

(9) It follows that a wise ruler is open to conviction, that is to say, he is open to argument and ready to change his view when it is shown to be wrong. On the other hand, an unwise ruler is obstinate—is not open to conviction—is not accessible to argument and will stick to the wrong conclusion.

Consult freely.

(10) It further follows that a wise ruler, in his anxiety to make sure that his conclusion is right, will, in matters of importance, freely consult his trustworthy and responsible counsellors and compare their conclusions with his own. On the other hand, an unwise ruler will think it beneath his dignity to consult such counsellors and will constantly run the risk of wrong conclusion and of all the mischief which must arise from the same.

Verify conclusions.

(11) One man, however able and experienced, cannot be sure of himself forming right conclusions in public affairs without consulting others. He may err in his fact; he may err in his reasoning; he may err from disregard of local conditions and circumstances. A dozen wrong conclusions may be found in any one case while there can be but one right conclusion. Hence it is necessary for every ruler, who is anxious to save his people from the evils of wrong conclusions, to verify his conclusion in every matter of importance by the means suggested above.

Success will arise by co-operation.

(12) Your Highness knows that I have dealt with the public affairs of important Native States for many years. I may venture to say that I have not been consciously wanting in care and diligence in dealing with important interests. Yet my experience has convinced me that I should make many serious errors of fact or of judgment, if I did not freely avail myself of the assistance of others. I am credited with some success in the management of the public affairs of the Native States concerned. Let me tell Your Highness that one great secret of that success is that I have tried to be guided by the principles and considerations above set forth. But my own is a very humble example. Your Highness may refer to persons immeasurably

higher and Your Highness will still find what I have said is true.

Hypocrisy.

(13) To stick to a wrong conclusion is really most culpable. Men are sometimes tempted to do so by the desire to appear firm. But it is no real firmness. It is spurious firmness. It is simple obstinacy. The public very soon discover this and blame the man concerned for obstinacy and hypocrisy.

Discuss conclusions quietly.

(14) The wisest course for a ruler is to take every possible precaution against wrong conclusions before acting on the same. Let those conclusions be made known, tested, discussed, and thoroughly settled in council. All this may be done very quietly and without the public knowing anything about it. The public judge by the results. If the results show that the ruler avoids wrong conclusions only, then the public praise him as a good ruler and will not care by what means the ruler does so. To sum up. By all possible means make sure of your conclusion being right, and then act firmly in respect to it. Firmness thus exercised is a great virtue in a ruler.

A ruler to be firm but kind (*a*) by patiently explaining to the party.

(15) Before concluding this part of the subject, I have to offer just a few further remarks. (*a*) Firmness, standing by itself, is one of the sterner virtues. Its harshness needs to be softened in

practice. A ruler should be firm, yet kind and considerate. Each case, as it occurs, must suggest how this object can be accomplished. It is a matter of habit and the habit may be acquired by care and attention. Generally, the harshness which is an element of firmness may be mitigated by patiently explaining matters to the party who considers himself aggrieved by your firmness. Let him see that your refusal to comply with his wishes is, by no means, due to your want of kindness, but due to the claims of justice, to the principles of government, to the force of precedents, or to some such other cause, which makes it your duty to act in the particular manner and which leaves you little or no option. If you yourself have not sufficient time to offer such explanations, you may easily direct the departmental head to do so.

(*b*) By obliging the party in some other legitimate manner.

(*b*) Another way in which the harshness of firmness may be mitigated is to try and oblige to some extent the party concerned in some other and legitimate manner. One example will suffice to make this clear. A certain public servant has become old and useless, and is, therefore, dispensed with. He comes and bitterly complains. I would not cause him to be rudely pushed out. I would hear him. Then I would explain to him how necessary it has become in these days that the administration should be efficient; how the administration would become inefficient if superannuated servants do not retire; that all of us must sooner or later become old and useless and give place to others; and so forth. And if the person concerned deserves the favour, I would offer to employ his son somewhere according to his merits. The great thing is to be firm yet sympathetic and obliging.

CHAPTER VI

ADVICE FROM OTHERS

Wednesday, July 1881.

Judge charitably of persons and acts.

The Maharaja's position is a very exalted one. His Highness will have to deal with many persons. He will have repeatedly to judge of persons and of their acts. His Highness will, therefore, do well to cultivate the important habit of judging charitably. Men's acts and motives present various aspects. The Maharaja will do well, as a rule, to prefer that aspect which is most favourable to the person concerned. In other words, if an act or motive is open to several interpretations, the Maharaja will do well to prefer that interpretation which is most in favour of the man concerned. In other words, again, place the most favourable constructions on men's acts and motives.

Because men may be presumed to prefer good to bad acts.

(2) The reason of this advice is that, except where the man concerned is known to be a bad man, men may be presumed to prefer good acts to bad

acts, and to prefer good motives to bad motives. This is a reasonable presumption arising from the natural state of things. It is a presumption dictated by justice and generosity, which ought always to characterize the highest personage in the country—I mean the Maharaja.

The Maharaja is then universally respected.

(3) Such presumption accords also with good policy. When the Maharaja judges in a charitable spirit as indicated above, men regard him all the more with respect and affection. They are positively grateful for the justice and generosity exercised towards them. Good men are pleased that the Maharaja avoids treating their acts and motives with injustice, and they become all the more anxious that their acts and motives should be good, and that they should thereby stand well in the estimation of so just and generous a master. If it should so happen that a bad man has been the object of the Maharaja's charitable view, even then the bad man feels ashamed and often changes his attitude and conduct for the better.

Examples: (*a*) the absence of a person from the Durbar.

(4) To make the matter further clear, I will here give some practical examples. (*a*) Suppose that an important officer or sirdar who had been invited to attend the Durbar, is found absent. The omission to attend the Durbar may possibly be at-

tributable to indifference, or to carelessness, or disrespect, or to sickness or accident or other unavoidable innocent cause. The principle I wish to impress on Your Highness ought to induce you to attribute the omission to some one of the unavoidable innocent causes rather than to some of those causes which imply blame on the part of the absentee officer or sirdar.

(b) The advice of a Minister.

(*b*) Again, a good Minister advises the Maharaja to yield some point to the British Resident. The advice may be attributable to good or bad motives. The Maharaja should attribute it to good motives rather than to bad motives.

(c) The advice of the Resident.

(*c*) Again, the Resident advises the Maharaja to undertake as little of judicial work as possible. The Maharaja should not attribute the advice to a desire on the part of the Resident to weaken the Maharaja, but should attribute it to his desire to save the Maharaja needless trouble and needless responsibilities.

(d) That of a Philosopher.

(*d*) Again, a political philosopher advises the Maharaja to make the machinery of his government, to the utmost extent, self-acting, self-regulating, and self-correcting. The Maharaja should attribute such advice to the best intentions towards himself and towards his people, and should not attribute it to a desire to make the Maharaja as powerless as possible.

(e) Of a friend.

(e) Again, a friend and councillor says to the Maharaja "such and such a person is an unprincipled and intriguing character. I would advise you to avoid that person." The Maharaja should attribute the advice to good intentions, and not to, say, selfish interest.

Smaller example: (a) theft of a jewel.

(5) Let us take now some smaller examples. (a) A jewel is stolen from the Palace. The Dewan institutes an active inquiry which involves the examination of even some personal attendants of the Maharaja. Perhaps the Dewan makes some of the servants concerned responsible for the value of the jewel, as a corrective of their carlessness and as a warning for the future. Such action should be presumed to be the result of the Dewan's wish to protect Palace jewellery from loss and it should not be presumed to be the result of any bad motives.

(b) Misbehaviour of a Mankari.

(b) Again, a Mankari misbehaves in a State-procession, draws his sword, and causes a disturbance. The Dewan takes due notice of it and does something by way of punishing the Mankari for such misbehaviour. The action should be attributed to good intentions and not to bad intentions. Many more similar examples might be given, such as occur daily in life; but it would be needless. The great thing is, as I have already said, that the Maharaja should cultivate the habit of interpreting men's acts and motives charitably, unless the man concerned is known to be a bad man.

Attribute an act to error rather than to mischief.

(6) The principle I am explaining generally requires also that, when an act is attributable to error or misapprehension on the one hand, or to deliberate mischievous intentions on the other, the Maharaja should prefer to assume the former rather than the latter. Such a habit of judging charitably is, as I have said above, a matter of justice and generosity and of good policy also. I may here add that it will be the means of conciliating people, and of avoiding the needless making of enemies. It will make the Maharaja's career smooth and agreeable. It will save the Maharaja's mind from constant irritation or painful suspicion, and secure it a calm composure and an elevated dignity, such as constitute one of the greatest ornaments of the throne. I feel quite sure that the cultivation of the habit I am speaking of, and its non-cultivation, will make a great difference in the happiness of the Maharaja.

It is a safeguard against intriguers.

(7) A Maharaja, who has succeeded in acquiring the excellent habit I am speaking of, will possess a great safeguard against intriguers. It must be remembered that an in-

triguer generally almost invariably puts the worst possible interpretation on the acts and motives of his enemies. But the Maharaja, who has acquired the excellent habit I am speaking of, will reject such uncharitable interpretations and prefer those which are charitable. Even if charitable interpretations do not readily suggest themselves, the good Maharaja will actually seek for such. He will actually try to conceive such.

Seek explanation from person affected.

(8) The principle of charitable interpretations I have been speaking of, will generally operate admirably when the Maharaja has to judge in a rough and ready manner, and to pass on to other matters. There may arise, however, important occasions for the Maharaja to determine, with some degree of certainty, which of the available interpretations is really applicable to a given case, especially when circumstances suggest an unfavourable interpretation. In such circumstances, it is a good rule, not to come, to an unfavourable conclusion until after giving the person affected a fair opportunity to afford any explanations in his power. The principle is, "do not condemn a man behind his back. Do not condemn him without hearing him."

Hear complaints of both parties.

(9) By way of illustration, suppose the Palace officer represents to the Maharaja that a certain expenditure which he (the officer) had incurred under the

orders of His Highness, is refused to be passed by the Auditor. The Palace officer may represent the matter in such a manner as to be quite disagreeable to His Highness, and as to induce His Highness to be displeased with the Auditor. But I say, do not be at once displeased with the Auditor without hearing what explanation the Auditor has to give. Let the Auditor be, in due course, called upon to explain why he declined to pass such expenditure. In nine cases, out of ten, the Auditor will give quite a satisfactory explanation. If however, the explanation is not satisfactory, then, and then alone, blame him.

Arrive at right conclusions.

(10) The course thus recommended will enable the Maharaja to avoid errors, and to arrive at right conclusions. It will enable him to do justice to his servants, public or private. It will inspire the servants themselves with confidence. Otherwise, they would feel that they are at the mercy of whims, caprices, and misrepresentations. All good servants should be made to feel that they would, on no account, incur the Maharaja's displeasure without real good cause.

Summary.

(11) To recapitulate briefly—

(*i*) When an act or motive is liable to several interpretations, the Maharaja should prefer that interpretation which is most favourable to the person affected.

(*ii*) If circumstances suggest that an unfavourable interpretation is the more probable one, the Maharaja should call for explanation from the person affected, and then judge.

CHAPTER VII

COMPROMISING SPIRIT.

14th September, 1881

Firmness to be controlled by prudence.

I have already explained what genuine firmness is, as distinguished from spurious firmness; and how useful the virtue is in rulers. But human affairs are such that it is not always possible or desirable to exercise firmness to its fullest extent; to exercise inflexible firmness. In rulers more especially, the exercise of one good quality has often to be controlled by other good qualities. Firmness has, for instance, to be controlled by prudence and circumspection.

Exercise a judicious spirit of compromise.

(2) Suppose A and B have much to do with each other in life. If, in any matter, A is determined to be so firm as to yield nothing to B, and B is determined to be so firm as to yield nothing to A, how can they get on at all? Difficulties and unpleasantness will ensue, and a dead-lock may be the result, or A and B will have to part; or some other serious mischief may be the consequence. It follows that firmness has sometimes to be judiciously relaxed with reference to the circumstances

of each case as it presents itself. When the firmness of one person encounters the firmness of another, some concession may have to be made for the sake of conciliation, peace and co-operation. In other words, some judicious compromise should be effected. The wisdom of a wise ruler is shown in exercising a judicious spirit of compromise. There are many instances of rulers gaining much by this spirit of compromise. On the other hand, there are also many instances of rulers losing much from want of this spirit.

Statesmanship is a series of compromises.

(3) It is quite certain that there is nothing disgraceful or derogatory in exercising a judicious spirit of compromise. In private life, every sensible man often exercises this spirit. In public life, the greatest men often exercise the same spirit. So much is this the case, that statesmanship is almost a series of compromises. No statesman expects to have his own way in all matters and at all times. All this must be well remembered lest a ruler should feel a false sense of humiliation, and refuse all compromise, and thereby draw down serious difficulties or dangers on himself. A ruler has often to give and take.

Avoid extremes.

(4) How far concessions should be made in any matter for the sake of effecting a compromise, is a question for judgment in each case. It will depend

on the strength of conviction, on the value of the principle at stake, on the force of the circumstances demanding concession and so forth. Concession much beyond the necessities of the case may be weakness; and refusing concessions up to the necessities of the case, and thereby incurring serious difficulties or dangers, may be unwisdom. The right mark must be hit. The loss arising from a proposed concession should be carefully weighed against the gain arising from the same; and if the scale incline to the latter, the concession may be made.

The stronger party to recognise the claims of reason.

(5) It may perhaps be briefly but usefully stated here that other things being equal, where concessions between governments are concerned, the weaker party may have to concede more than the stronger. But the disparity, in this respect, is diminished in proportion as the stronger party recognizes the claims of reason, justice and liberality as superior to the advantages conferred by mere might.

Importance of the compromising spirit.

(6) Without a judicious compromising spirit, individuals would make families unhappy, statesmen would make nations unhappy, and kings and rulers would make the world unhappy. The foregoing considerations need to be fully kept in view, and they should be allowed to modify to the necessary degree the exercise of the quality of firmness.

CHAPTER VIII

Maharaja's Absence

28th September 1881

It is desirable that, except for occasional travelling, or on the ground of ill-health, the Maharaja should not needlessly leave his territories, and spend his time outside. Some persons may recommend to His Highness to go to Matheran or some other locality outside, and spend the summer there. Other persons may similarly recommend to His Highness to go somewhere else and spend the winter there. The cold weather with its festivities may in its turn tempt His Highness to leave his territories. But the subjects of Native States do not at all like their Maharaja's absence in these ways. They wish to see their Maharaja living in their midst and spending his share of the revenues in the country itself. They wish to see His Highness constantly among them, looking after their welfare. It is natural for them to dislike their ruler leaving country and people in search of personal pleasure.

The Maharaja should spend as much time as possible in his State.

(2) Moreover, a Native Prince attended with a large retinue is not generally welcome at places of resort by the European community. Disturbance to sanitation and to public convenience is apprehended, and hence restrictions come to be imposed, by no means agreeable to the Native Prince. There are the other restrictions about carrying arms and ammunition. Disagreeable questions arise about the Prince and his followers paying tolls and other municipal taxes. Difficult or delicate questions arise as to the relations of the Prince and followers with the British Police, Magistracy and Courts. Suits are apt to be preferred even when supplies and carriage have been fairly paid for.

The several restrictions, while travelling.

(3) Considering all this and also considering that the residence of the Maharaja outside his territories leads to great extra expense without the least benefit to His Highness' subjects, it seems clear that His Highness should not needlessly absent himself often from his country.

The extra expense without any benefit to the State.

CHAPTER IX

Fame

The Maharaja should not be in a hurry to become famous. Fame, as a good and benevolent ruler, is indeed a legitimate and laudable object of a ruler's ambition. Nothing is more gratifying in this world to noble natures than being recognized as the benefactors of communities. But such fame requires time to achieve. It is the reward of long years of the purest intentions, of the highest disinterestedness, of patient and careful study, and of sustained and arduous exertions for the public good. There is no short cut to such fame. The ruler who sufficiently realizes these facts will avoid an unnatural and feverish activity which would inconsiderately meddle with many re-settled things—meddle merely for the sake of notoriety. He will pursue an even course steadily and smoothly.

No short cut to fame. It is the reward of patience.

(2) That ruler would soon make himself miserable who hungers after applause every day and at every step. The world has too much business of its own to spare

No hungering after applause.

time to applaud its rulers so often. Nor would the world be acting wisely to make its applause so cheap as to be given on trivial occasions.

Accounts of hired flatterers end in failure.

(3) A ruler, who would not wait, but is impatient to get fame, sometimes employs puffing in the newspapers. Hired flatterers write long accounts of the most trifling acts of the ruler and invite the public to admire his bottomless wisdom and benevolence in every movement of his. But such attempts to force fame soon end, as they ought to end, in signal failure. A discerning public does not require a long time to discover the false or exaggerated claim urged by mercenary advocates.

Deserve fame.

(4) The best advice, therefore, to young rulers is—Do good steadily, constantly and unostentatiously. Thus deserve Fame, and leave it to come when it will ; come it will in the end.

CHAPTER X

PERSONAL PLEADINGS BY VAKILS

19th October 1881

Should Vakils plead before the Maharaja?

The Maharaja may occasionally have to enter into the merits of cases with a view to satisfy himself that justice has been done. This is all right and proper. But the question arises, whether His Highness is to allow Vakils, Mooktiars, Lawyers, etc., to appear before him personally and to plead the cause of their clients.

No.

(2) It is not desirable that His Highness should allow such a proceeding. Even the Governor-General and the Governor do not allow it. The reasons are cogent. In the first place, the Maharaja could not at all spare time to hear professional pleaders. In the next place, it would hardly suit the dignity of His Highness' exalted position. Again, it would subject His Highness to grave difficulties and embarrassments. It will, therefore, be desirable to let it be known, on the first occasion which may present itself, that His Highness will not allow personal pleadings before him. This position will have to be maintained with great firmness.

Judge from the record of the case.

(3) The principle should be that His Highness judges for himself from the record of the case which must include the pleadings on both sides. The parties have already had opportunities to set forth their respective facts and arguments, and they cannot bring in fresh matter at the last stage.

Parties to be heard in special cases.

(4) As a general rule, neither vakils nor even the parties themselves should have the right to be heard by the Maharaja. If in any special case it pleases His Highness to do so, His Highness may send for the parties and give them a hearing. This appears to be the safest, most convenient, and most dignified position.

CHAPTER XI

DEPUTATIONS

16th November 1881

The Maharaja has to be very careful in receiving deputations personally. If His Highness be known to be disposed to receive, deputations would endlessly demand interviews with him—deputations from sections of his own subjects, deputations from neighbouring cities and towns, deputations from Bombay and Poona, and deputations from even more distant communities. They would present long addresses and make long speeches. They would even enter into troublesome discussions and expect His Highness to make definite replies. They would embarrass His Highness with matters civil, religious, political, aesthetical, and what not. And whatever His Highness says to them or even does not say to them, would be publicly criticised with unsparing severity.

Every deputation not to be received by the Maharaja.

(2) As a general rule, therefore, let the ordinary deputations be referred to the Ministers of His Highness. If, for instance, a deputation has to make a representation on a revenue matter, let it go to the head of the Revenue Department.

Ordinary deputations to be referred to the Ministers.

If a deputation has to make a representation on an educational matter, let it go to the head of the Educational Department. And so on. The head of the department concerned will receive the deputations, fully hear them, and do whatever may be necessary or desirable. In important matters the deputation may go to the Dewan or Chief Minister. This appears to be the best and the most convenient course where the deputation has to do with matters of business.

In important cases consult the Dewan.

(3) His Highness may consent to receive the deputation personally, only when the matter, or occasion, or the deputation itself, is very important. Such cases must be rare, and may be distinguished from the others by some consultation with the Dewan.

The Dewan to be previously informed of its nature.

(4) Even in such rare cases, the Dewan should be previously informed of the nature and object of the deputation. The Dewan should see the address or representation to be preferred by the deputation, in order that he may be enabled to prepare His Highness for the same.

The reply to be cautiously framed and its preparation to be entrusted to responsible Ministers.

(5) His Highness' replies to deputations must be carefully and cautiously framed. When the reply can be clear and specific, let it, by all means, be so. But it often happens that a clear and specific reply cannot be immediately

given by His Highness. The matter requires to be maturely considered hereafter. If so, His Highness' reply should not commit His Highness to any opinion or action prematurely or incautiously. The reply should raise no hopes—much less make any promises such as it might be difficult or embarrassing to fulfil hereafter. In short, such replies require much judgment and tact. It is not any person who merely knows to write the language correctly, that can properly prepare such replies. His Highness will do well to entrust the preparation of such replies to his responsible Ministers. Even European sovereigns follow this course.

CHAPTER XII

Taking Counsel

1st December 1881

Some weeks ago when we met here, I dwelt at some length on the importance, and indeed the necessity, of the Maharaja's taking counsel in all matters of public importance, the great object in view being to reach right conclusions for the purposes of good government.

The object is to arrive at right conclusions.

(2) The question arises, whose counsel is the Maharaja to take ? Surely not the counsel of anybody or of everybody. Scores of people are ready to undertake the honour of giving advice to the Maharaja in any and in every matter. And the most ignorant men are perhaps the most forward in this respect, because they are seldom troubled with doubts and difficulties.

Whose counsel should the Maharaja take.

(3) The Maharaja has to exercise care and judgment in the choice of his counsellors. This is one of the greatest and imperative duties of His Highness. This is one of the most essential conditions of his success as a ruler.

Select the counsellors with care.

(4) The Maharaja should exercise care and judgment to choose advisers possessing mainly the following qualifications :—

The necessary qualifications.

(*a*) Knowledge of the theory or of the principles or of the science of the business to be done.

(*a*) A real knowledge.

(*b*) Practical experience which shows how that knowledge is to be applied and which supplies details.

(*b*) Practical experience.

(*c*) Love of truth, justice and disinterestedness as supplying the best motives.

(*c*) Love of truth.

(5) Let the Maharaja firmly grasp these qualifications, and choose advisers possessing these qualifications, and he will thereby prove to the world that he himself possesses ability and judgment. There is no doubt that the Maharaja's reputation and success as a ruler depend, in no small measure, upon the right choice of his advisers.

Grasp these qualifications firmly.

(6) It follows that the Maharaja need not seek advice from persons who do not possess the qualifications summarised above. Any advice coming from such persons would be of little value. On the contrary, it might be positively mischievous. If, therefore, any such

Don't seek advice from others.

persons volunteer their advice to His Highness, as they are often too apt to do, His Highness will do well not to pay much attention to the same. Indeed, it would be waste of time and attention even to listen much to such advice; and any serious consultations held by the Maharaja with such persons might only lower His Highness in the estimation of the enlightened public, and might have the further effect of shaking the confidence of His Highness' real well-wishers in His Highness' judgment; for, these well-wishers would say—or at least think—"The Maharaja does not seem to be able to distinguish between competent and incompetent advisers. Hence it is a mere chance whose advice will prevail."

Do not over-rule wise advice.

(7) I have dwelt at some length on this topic, because there are instances—indeed there are too many instances in Native States—in which the soundest and the wisest advice has been over-ruled by the advice of an intriguing Karkoon, and even by that of a mere Jasood, or of a narrow-minded priest, or of a clever musician. It is thus that some Native States have been misgoverned, and others have been ruined.

Avoid incompetent advisers.

(8) By digesting and remembering the hints given above, the Maharaja will be able to relieve himself from the distractions of a crowd of incompetent advisers who

abound in Native Courts (Palaces) and who seek every possible opportunity to offer and even to press their advice. The Maharaja getting clear of incompetent advisers is a grand condition to begin with. Before, then, the Maharaja seeks or accepts any particular person's advice in any matter, let His Highness ask himself these questions:—Does the person possess some theoretical and practical knowledge of that matter, and is he known to be a lover of truth, justice and disinterestedness? If the questions can be answered in the affirmative, the person in question is a competent adviser. If the questions cannot be answered in the affirmative, then the person in question is not a competent adviser.

How if advisers differ.

(9) Let us suppose now that the Maharaja has successfully learnt how to choose competent advisers. If these competent advisers all agree and give the same advice to the Maharaja, well and good. But the question arises, what is the Maharaja to do if these competent advisers disagree, and give conflicting advice? The Maharaja may, at any time, be placed in this position, and it is very desirable that His Highness should know how to proceed.

Then Judge carefully.

(10) When differing or conflicting advice is given by competent advisers, it will manifestly devolve on the Maharaja himself to carefully judge, which advice should be

selected as the best for adoption. This is a great function of the Maharaja and must be performed with intelligence as well as with care.

Prefer the advice of a responsible officer.

(11) I offer the following hints which may be of considerable use to His Highness in performing this great and necessary function. The choice of the best advice must be made on a combined view of several considerations, the chief of which I proceed to submit. Give decided preference to the advice which is given by the responsible officer over the advice which is given by an irresponsible individual. The latter, however able and conscientious, is not generally in the position in which the former is for judging correctly. A full sense of responsibility—a full sense of the loss of reputation, etc., which might be entailed in consequence of having given unsound advice to the Maharaja—forms a great security for sound advice, a security which must be wanting or must be imperfect in the instance of an irresponsible individual.

His advice to be in writing.

(12) In order to obtain the full benefit of this security, the Maharaja may, on important occasions, well ask that the advice given him may be committed to writing in the shape of a memo. giving the reasons for that advice and bearing date and signature. It is a matter of experience that many a person who

gives evidence without much thought and in an off-hand manner in oral communication, feels a far greater and clearer sense of responsibility when called upon to record that advice. Whatever he records will be more deliberate, more clear and more precise than what he merely speaks.

Prefer the advice of an expert.

(13) Again when, the subject of the advice is one of general principles, prefer the advice of that person who is best versed in those principles. Similarly, when the subject of the advice is one of practical experience, prefer the advice of that person who most possesses such experience.

And that of the majority.

(14) Again, subject to the other considerations, that advice which the majority of competent and responsible advisers give should be preferred to that which the minority may give.

A few important considerations.

(15) Again, subject to the other considerations, prefer that advice which least disturbs the existing state of things. Again, subject to the other considerations, prefer that advice which least opposes the sentiments and wishes of the people. Again, similarly prefer that advice which is most in conformity with the course followed by a good neighbouring Government, especially by the British

Government. Again, similarly prefer that advice which the Government of India is more likely to approve of in the interests of this state. The foregoing are important guiding considerations, all or some of which will enable the Maharaja to decide which advice he should consider the best for his adoption.

Weigh the considerations for and against.

(16) The most perplexing case will be that in which all the foregoing considerations do not tell the same way, but some tell in favour of, and some against, a given measure. In such a case, the considerations for and against must be carefully weighed, and the Maharaja's decision should be according to the balance struck. How the considerations for and against should be weighed, and how the balance should be struck, it would be difficult to say exactly. It is a matter of habit and practice.

The advisers to discuss in the Maharaja's presence.

(17) It will often better enable the Maharaja to decide correctly if his competent and responsible advisers be made to discuss their differences freely in His Highness' presence. His Highness himself may take some part in the descussion and put questions in reference to the grounds of preference set forth above. Such a discussion may result in all reconciling their differences and reaching a common conclusion.

(18) If, however, a common conclusion is not arrived at, and if the Maharaja finds that he cannot, with confidence, *strike a clear balance* of consideration as above suggested, then the safest course may be, if possible, to postpone the matter altogether for future consideration and decision. At some future time, the way becomes more clear.

In the absence of a comon conclusion, postpone the matter.

(19) If, however, the posponement of the matter be not possible and circumstances require some immediate decision, then, the safest course for His Highness will probably be to trust to his responsible Chief Minister's advice above that of all others.

Or trust to the Chief Minister.

CHAPTER XIII

WORK

7th December 1881.

Moderation of work necessary.

A Maharaja ought not to overburden himself with work. He ought not to undertake so much work that his health would suffer thereby, that his recreations would be cut off or reduced, and that the work itself could not be done with that knowledge and deliberation which are necessary for its proper performance.

The Maharaja has to work all his life.

(2) It is to be remembered that the Maharaja has to work all his life. It is not as if he should work very hard for a few years and then retire from business. This circumstance, all the more, imposes moderation of work.

Work about four hours.

(3). Roughly speaking, the Maharaja should have work for not more than four or five hours per diem. This will leave time for health, for recreation, for study, for family and social duties and pleasures. Whenever there is special extra business, His Highness may especially devote extra time to the same.

Do not do everything yourself.

(4). A great number of details His Highness may well devolve on his ministers. In respect to these, instead of His Highness passing orders in each individual case, His Highness may well give some general orders which will apply to whole groups of cases. This course will save time and labour. The principle should be that His Highness should not burden himself with such work as he can get others to do equally well. His Highness' position is like that of an engineer. The engineer need not himself turn every wheel in the engine. On the contrary the more skilful the engineer, the more successful is he in arranging that the engine shall do the greatest amount of work so as to leave him abundant time to supervise the whole and to devise important improvements.

CHAPTER XIV

HOW TO AVOID WORRY

Necessity of protecting against worry.

For the preservation of the Maharaja's physical and intellectual health, it is very necessary that His Highness should protect himself against the terrible worry to which he would certainly be constantly exposed, if he were not to take the requisite precautions.

How worry may arise.

(2) Numberless individuals are apt to pester His Highness with pressing solicitations for favours of various sorts. These may be mainly particularised as follows :—

(*a*) Solicitation for appointments, promotions, increase of pay, and transfers from one place to another.

(*b*) Solicitation for granting of Nemnooks, for their increase, or restoration of Nemnooks, resumed or reduced.

(*c*) Solicitation for granting of Warshasans, for their increase, or restoration of Warshasans, resumed or reduced.

(*d*) Solicitation for presents of jewellery, Poshaks, money for marriages.

(*e*) Solicitation for Seedhas.

(*f*) Solicitation for loan of carriages, horses, sowars, &c.

(*g*) Solicitation for loans of money, advance payment, of Nemnooks, &c.

(*h*) Solicitation to set aside, alter or re-open decisions already given.

(*i*) Solicitation for religious and charitable grants or contributions. And so forth.

General principles to avoid worry.

(3) A great proportion of the worry thus arising may be avoided by remembering and pleading a few general principles. These may be briefly stated here.

(*a*) Non interference with the heads of departments.

(*a*) In those cases in which His Highness has given power to the heads of departments to act, His Highness may, as a rule, refuse to interfere. This is only right and proper.

(*b*) Applicant to be asked to apply through the proper channel.

(*b*) In many cases His Highness may, as a rule, tell the applicant that he should apply through the head of the department concerned.

(*c*) Inability to increase expenditure.

(*c*). In some cases His Highness may say that he is unable, as a rule, to increase the existing limits of expenditure, as it is most important that the expenditure should be kept below the income as at present.

(d) Past dakhlas to be applied.

(*d*). In numerous cases the limits of past dakhlas may be applied to.

(e) The impropriety of re-opening a matter once decided.

(*e*). In others, the principle may be enforced that, when a matter has once been fairly considered and decided, it cannot be allowed to be re-opened, unless upon fresh and cogent ground.

CHAPTER XV

JUDGMENT

Men who are in a high position and exercise great power,—especially rulers—need to cultivate, constantly, the habit of judgment. It is the habit of weighing reasons on the one side and on the other, and striking the balance. It is a most necessary and useful habit, and may be acquired by making an earnest effort.

Cultivate habit of judgment.

(2) Whenever anything has to be preferred out of several things let not the preference be arbitrarily or capriciously made. The preference should be made for some good reason. This principle applies to small as well as to great matters. In short, on every occasion, let reason assert its sway. Any ruler who constantly walks under the guidance of reason will walk a safe path.

Let reason be your guide.

(3) If any one recommend anything to the ruler, let the ruler ask for the reasons for the recommendation. By doing everything according to reason, the ruler is greatly strengthened; because all reasonable

Ask for reasons.

men take his side. He commands the sympathy and support of his subjects and of the general public.

Greater success is achieved by better judgment.

(4) In fact it is the capacity of judgment which makes the greatest difference between one man and another. Given any two men in similar circumstances, that man will generally achieve the greater success who has the better judgment.

The quality of judgment to be patiently cultivated by daily reading.

(5) But the judgment is not an intuitive quality. It requires to be patiently and constantly cultivated. Its right exercise also requires the possession of a large stock of sound general principles. It is further desirable to study how men of acknowledged eminence judge in difficult or intricate matters. A part of daily reading may, therefore, be very advantageously directed to this end.

CHAPTER XVI

PROPOSALS

Exhaustive consideration of any proposal.

Whenever anything is proposed for his consideration, His Highness will do well to consider how that thing will affect

(*a*) himself,

(*b*) his own subjects,

(*c*) the subjects of other States,

(*d*) the British Government,

(*e*) the general public, and

(*f*) all cases of the same sort occurring hereafter.

It is in this manner that the consideration should be exhaustively gone through in matters of importance.

The cardinal principle: Do to others as we should wish to be done by.

(2) One other important test of a measure is to consider how we should like it if others adopted such a measure. This has reference to the cardinal principle of doing to others as we should wish to be done by. What I mean is that the bearing of a given measure on the several interests concerned should be fully examined, and it should be examined in regard to the immediate present and in regard to the future.

(3) Some Maharajas are very fond of wishing to make some alteration or other in any proposal placed before them to make the alteration merely for the sake of making one, such a disposition needs to be guarded against. It is a disposition likely to impede the progress of business.

Disposition to alter proposals not desirable.

(4) The disposition has its origin generally in petty vanity. The owner of the disposition supposes that he displays the superiority of his wisdom by making some alteration in the proposal before him. But this is, of course, a mistake. Any and every alteration cannot be a proof of superior wisdom. It is only when an alteration is supported by valid reason, that it implies superiority. On the other hand, when an alteration is made without valid reason, and when it is made merely to lead other people to inferior or superior wisdom, it is the result of positive weakness. People soon discover the weakness. They distinguish the pretence from the reality.

Every alteration not proof of superior wisdom.

(5) The Maharaja may, to any extent, scrutinise the proposal before him. He may discuss it. He may suggest objections and obtain explanations. He may alter the proposal when he feels satisfied that there are good reasons for an alteration. But, what is to be strongly deprecated is, insisting upon alterations

Alter when necessary.

merely for the paltry motive of asserting superiority or power.

Do not be guided by flatterers.

(6) Such a motive is not chimerical; for I have seen it existing and operating; and I have seen it fostered and stimulated by flatterers, from whom few palaces are altogether free.

Trust the officers for details.

(7) That Maharaja greatly facilitates business who has the strength of mind firmly to say, "I concur," when he is satisfied in the main, and when he may trust his officers in regard to details. This is the only way to prevent a block of business and to realise sufficient leisure for His Highness to deal with the more important questions worthy of his attention.

CHAPTER XVII

(A) MEANS FOR SUCCESS

To do anything well and successfully, the first necessary condition is to get a clear conception of the end to be accomplished. What is the specific end to be accomplished and what is not? These questions should be put and unequivocally answered.

Get a clear conception of the end in view.

(2) This being done, the next consideration should be directed to the choice of the means. There may be a variety of means to accomplish the end in view. Which of these means is the best? Determine this as carefully as possible.

Consider the best means.

(3) Having selected the best means, consider and forecast all the possible difficulties and accidents which might occur to disturb or defeat the object in view, and adopt or be prepared with the necessary measures to prevent or counteract such difficulties and accidents.

The possible difficulties.

(4) Then proceed with the undertaking with due regard to time, place, and circumstances. If such a course is pursued, success will be maximised; that is to say, success will be attained in the majority of cases.

Other considerations for attaining success.

(5) Simple and almost obvious as is the course above suggested, many persons neglect it or adopt it more or less imperfectly. It is the degree of attention given to the course above indicated which mainly makes the difference between one man and another in regard to their success in their careers. The person who pays full attention to the course is seldom taken by surprise. He simply goes through a carefully pre-arranged programme. On the other hand, the person who acts otherwise proceeds loosely, and is exposed to confusion and discomfiture at the several stages of the given undertaking.

Give full attention to the course.

(6) The remarks I have offered apply to all persons in general, but they apply especially to rulers who have continually to act, and who have often to act in important matters.

The remarks specially applicable to rulers.

(b) Treatment of High Officers.

Assuming that high officers have been carefully selected for their capacity and probity, the Maharaja should treat them with confidence. It would be unjust and impolitic to suspect them of a disposition to misrepresent matters to His Highness, or to misguide His Highness in disposing of the same. A Maharaja who has not learnt how to repose confidence in others, will be able to accomplish but

Treat officers with confidence.

little in his career, because he will not secure cordial co-operation.

Preserve their self-respect.

(2) The self-respect of the high officers should be preserved and strengthened by His Highness treating them with courtesy and consideration.

To err is human.

(3) Men perfect in every human quality, are not to be found in this world. Some imperfections may always be found in the most gifted. His Highness should make generous allowance for this manifest truth. Take the man as a whole—

> Be to his faults a little blind,
> Be to his virtues very kind.

Allow free discussions.

(4) Let every high officer be permitted to freely discuss matters and especially to express differences of opinion.

Do not speak ill of him behind his back.

(5) As a rule, abstain from speaking unfavourably of the high officer behind his back. Every unfavourable remark would be noted and printed abroad, and people would soon cease to feel that respect for him without which he could hardly fulfil his duties properly.

Nor allow him to be abused.

(6) For similar reasons, do not permit common persons, who frequent native courts, to abuse high officers of the State in a light and reckless manner.

(7) Also, do not admit petitions which speak of high officers in needlessly disrespectful terms.

Do not admit petitions against them.

(8) If there is occasion for His Highness to say anything unpleasant to a high officer, better say it to him privately than while others are present.

Make remarks privately.

(9) In short, let the country see that the Maharaja and his high officers form a coherent and compact body with all the strength which arises from identity of motives, sentiments and actions.

The ruler and the officers form one compact body.

(10) I have advised that the Maharaja should not overwork himself. His Highness should also see that his high officers are not over-worked. Let them have time for health, study and some recreation. They will do all the better service for being thus taken care of.

The high officers not to be over-worked.

CHAPTER XVIII

Good Faith

Good faith is absolutely necessary in the conduct of public affairs. It is even more necessary in the conduct of public than of private affairs. It may be generally affirmed that every virtue is even more necessary to a Government than to an individual, because the effects of Governmental action are immensely more extensive.

Good faith necessary in public affairs.

(2) Good faith particularly requires that promises made should be made with the sincere desire to fulfil them, and promises made should be faithfully fulfilled.

Promises should be fulfilled.

(3) I am sorry to say that this principle has not been sufficiently attended to in many Native States. What is the consequence? The promises of Native States are not sufficiently believed in, not even the most deliberate and solemn promises.

The consequence of breach of promise.

(4) How this matter stands in Native States and in British India may be realised and measured by means of one illustration. Suppose a Native State announces a loan to the public—that is to say,

Illustration: the public lending money to Government.

the Native State desires to borrow money from the public. Suppose the British India Government similarly announces a loan, it is certain that the public will rush to the British Government with funds, but not so to the Native State. The Native State may offer even a higher rate of interest; yet the public will generally prefer to lend money to the British Government at lower interest. Why this great difference? Because the public feel that the British Government will faithfully perform its promises, whereas they do not feel so to the same degree as regards the Native State.

Promises not to be recklessly made.

(5) Public ease, security and confidence, and public progress and prosperity, require that the Maharaja should scrupulously fulfil the promises he may make to individuals or to the community. But this again requires that promises should not be recklessly made. Before any promise is made, let there be full enquiry and full deliberation.

CHAPTER XIX

REWARDS

The Maharaja should not be extravagant and indiscriminate in giving rewards, but he ought neither to be parsimonious nor too discriminating. He should be just and liberal. To be so is a public duty because it promotes public good.

Extravagance and parsimony.

(2) Rewards are pecuniary or honorary, or both combined. Their object is to confer pleasure and to stimulate useful service. It follows that he who bestows rewards should take care that this fundamental object is fulfilled—that the reward proposed in a given case is adequate enough to confer pleasure and discriminating enough to stimulate useful service.

Rewards stimulate useful service.

(3) The ordinary pay which a servant draws is his remuneration for ordinary service, therefore no special reward need be granted. Indeed, it might even prove mischievous to grant special rewards for ordinary service. The question of reward

No special rewards for ordinary service.

should be entertained only if service beyond that ordinarily expected, has been rendered.

No rewards for little or no service.

(4) *A fortiori* it follows that no rewards should be granted where there has been little or no service of any kind rendered. I mention this because there are not wanting in Baroda, persons who expect special and liberal rewards because they have incurred large debts, because they belong to old families, and so forth.

A small difference may be sacrificed, to obtain the reputation of liberality.

(5) In matters of pecuniary reward, whether the Maharaja gets the reputation of liberality or parsimony, turns in a proportion of cases on comparatively small differences. A policeman does some extraordinary good service. Give him a reward of 75 rupees, it is deemed stingy. Give him 100 rupees, it is liberal ; the difference being only 25 rupees. Take another example. A worthy officer retires from the public service. Give him a gratuity of 9 month's pay, it may be stingy. Give him a gratuity of 12 months' pay, it is liberal, the difference being only three months' pay. Again, a Poshak is to be presented. If it be of the value of 200 rupees, it looks stingy. If it be of the value of 300 rupees, it looks liberal, in such cases, the comparatively small difference may be sacrificed in order that His Highness may acquire the reputation of liberality.

(6) Similar remarks apply to rewards in the shape of expressions of approbation and praise. These should be adequate and even generous.

Expressions of approbation.

(7) One good test of the adequacy and liberality of a reward, in any case, is that the recipient of the reward should not be ashamed to show it to others. On the contrary, he should be able to show it with pride and gratification. It is only then that it operates as a stimulant and fulfils the object of reward.

The recipient to be proud of the reward.

(8) A Maharaja who judiciously exercises the power of rewarding immensely increases his influence for good.

Judicious exercise of the power.

CHAPTER XX

POWER OF PARDON

His Highness has the power of pardoning. This power is generally known as the prerogative of mercy. But it is to be remembered that no power whatever should be arbitrarily exercised.

The prerogative of mercy not to be arbitrarily exercised.

(2) What then, are the principles which should govern the exercise of His Highness' clemency ?

A few principles.

(*a*) His Highness cannot grant a pardon until after the person concerned has been tried and convicted. In other words it is only a convicted criminal that His Highness can pardon. In other words, again, His Highness cannot say " Do not try this person, for I have pardoned him." Nor can His Highness say while the trial is going on, " Stop the trial of this person, for I have pardoned him."

(*a*) Only a convicted criminal can be pardoned.

(*b*) What I have just stated is one important principle. Another is that His Highness cannot arbitrarily pardon any criminal he pleases. In short, there must be apparently some good reason for clemency. For instance, that the court concerned

(*b*) There must be some reason for clemency.

has manifestly misjudged the evidence and wrongly convicted the prisoner; or that, since the termination of the trial, some new evidence has come to light showing the innocence of the prisoner or making his guilt doubtful.

(c) Consult the Judges.

(c) In practice, it is desirable, though not imperative, to consult the Judges before His Highness grants pardon. They will be able to assist with their opinion as to whether the prisoner deserves pardon or not in the given circumstances. The opinion of the Judges is entitled to much weight though it is not binding upon His Highness.

The same principle to be applied to mitigating and commuting punishments.

(3) His Highness has also the power of mitigating or commuting punishments awarded. The exercise of this power, too, is governed by considerations similar to those above stated. I will only add that this power may be exercised where the sentences passed are harsh or over-severe in reference to the youth, or the sex, or the rank of the prisoner, or other circumstance denoting extraordinary sensibility.

The practice of pardoning convicts on occasions of rejoicing not desirable yet care to be exercised.

(4) On occasions of extraordinary public rejoicing a certain limited number of convicts are sometimes pardoned and liberated. As this is a questionable practice, it must not be frequently adopted. It is not very

clear why, when the Maharaja has reason to rejoice he, the great guardian of the security of life, person and property, should to any extent weaken that security by letting loose on society a number of proved delinquents. If such a thing is to be done, it must be done on very rare and extraordinary occasions; and even then, great and intelligent care should be taken to select such convicts for pardon, as are most likely to abstain from offending after release. For instance, convicts may be selected whose offences have not been very heinous, or have been the results of misfortune, and who have suffered at least one-half of the punishments awarded to them.

Refer to old precedents.

(5) In this respect, the principles which have guided us during these six years may be referred to with advantage as precedents. They will be found recorded.

CHAPTER XXI

Respect for Others' Feelings

Every Ruler—every person who has to deal much with men—should always be careful to respect the feelings of others. Nothing needlessly harsh or offensive or unpleasant should be said or done in matters, whether great or small. This is a most useful and honourable habit which is well worth the trouble it requires to acquire it. Observation and study are required for its acquisition.

Respect others' feelings.

(2) One easy way of prejudging what might be harsh, or offensive or unpleasant, is to imagine how we should feel if others said or did that to ourselves. Many do not act on this principle well, but so many do not act on this principle in practice.

How we should feel if others did that to us.

(3) Another help towards acquiring the habit in question is to watch the thoughts, words and deeds of men who are distinguished for having successfully acquired that habit.

Watch those who respect others.

CHAPTER XXII

Newspaper Opinions

Because any opinion appears in print in the newspapers, it does not follow that it is correct. The real value of the opinion expressed depends upon the respectability of the newspaper and of the writer concerned. Not unfrequently we find this by no means very high. Persons of very imperfect knowledge or judgment sometimes take to writing in the newspapers. Sometimes, persons of very inferior probity do the same. Sometimes, persons supposing themselves to be injured or slighted, write in the journals in the disguise of disinterested observers or critics. And persons are not altogether wanting who sell their opinions—that is to say, publish opinions to order according to money paid.

They are not always correct.

(2) In these circumstances, we have to be very careful as to what weight should be attached to newspaper opinions and criticism.

Do not attach much weight.

Papers honestly conducted not to be disregarded.

(3) Newspapers honestly conducted and representing public opinion, or expressing the ideas of honest and intelligent thinkers, should not be disregarded. On the contrary, they should be read and considered as material aids to good government.

CHAPTER XXIII

PRIVATE STUDY

The Maharaja's studies will not, I trust, be discontinued after assuming power. It, is most important that they should be continued on some fixed plan. A large portion of His Highness' time and attention will, of course, have to be devoted to official business. Yet time should be found for private study —say about three hours every day.

Do not neglect private study.

(2) The objects to be aimed at in this direction are (*a*) His Highness should increase his knowledge of the English language, (*b*) of useful truths.

The object of study.

(3) The English language being foreign to us and otherwise difficult, we have to exercise ourselves constantly in it. If not, we not only do not improve, but we go back. We must read a great deal of good English every day. We must also speak and write the language every day to some extent. The main object of knowing the English language is to acquire a knowledge of useful truths. Therefore our reading should be made the means of also augmenting our stock of truths.

Speak and write the English language.

Plan of study.

(4) All these things being clear, my esteemed friend Mr. Elliot will, no doubt, suggest to His Highness a somewhat detailed plan of studies.

(a) Perusal of newspapers.

(*a*) The plan will, doubtless, include the regular perusal of some well-conducted newspapers. His Highness should follow the current history of the world generally and of India and England in particular. I mean that large facts should not be missed.

(b) Speeches of Statesmen.

(*b*) The speeches of great statesmen like Mr. Gladstone may be read with advantage when they relate to matters of wider than local importance.

(c) Parliamentary Debates.

(*c*) The debates in Parliament, when they relate to such matters, will also repay perusal.

(d) Histories of Native States.

(*d*) Almost everything which relates to the Native States of India should be read and noted. The Viceroy's speeches on such matters must not escape notice.

(e) Blue books.

(*e*) Parliamentary Blue Books relating to Indian affairs may be regularly got out, and useful portions read.

(f) Administration reports.

(*f*) The Annual Administration Report of the Bombay Government should be a book familiar to His Highness.

Vast readings bring large ideas.

(5) Much of this sort of reading will have a great bearing on His Highness' public

duties, and will strengthen His Highness' powers to perform those duties. The reading should be such as to bring His Highness' mind into contact with large ideas and elevated sentiments, and to counteract the cramping influences of the ordinary company which is to be had in the Palace. The great danger to which Native Princes are exposed is that they are liable to limit themselves to such company whereby their ideas get dwarfed or contracted. They confine themselves to a narrow and fossilised world which shuts out the higher lights of a progressive age. The best antidote to this is that they should make themselves conversant with the thoughts of the most enlightened of mankind.

Read biograpnies and good novels.

(6) His Highness' reading may occasionally embrace some biographies and novels calculated to inspire high ideal of human excellence.

Maintain a high ideal of life.

(7) To maintain a high ideal of life and duty in an exalted station and in the exercise of great power, requires considerable moral force, and this moral force stands in need of constant renovation in some way like that suggested.

CHAPTER XXIV

CONCLUDING ADVICE

I have thus brought the minor hints to a close. These hints also will be found to be more or less, useful to the Maharaja in practical administration. What I have communicated under both the major and the minor heads will, I hope, serve like a small compass which, though small, shows the broad line to be followed in navigation.

These hints will be useful in practical administration.

(2) Theoretical knowledge alone, however, is not sufficient in the government of human beings. To such knowledge must be constantly added the benefit of actual practical experience. I am anxious that His Highness should not be led to under-value practical experience and thereby to under-estimate the desirableness of consulting practical men in important matters as they arise. Let me here give an illustration which will impress the material difference between theory and practice. His Highness knows well how to write with his right hand. So far as the theory of writing is concerned, the left hand is quite equal to the right hand. And yet, let His Highness try to write

Theoretical knowledge to be supplemented by practical experience.

with his left hand, and he will see that he can do it very imperfectly or perhaps not at all. Why ? The theory is all right with respect to both hands, but the right hand has had the benefit of practice which the left hand has not had. Mark the immense difference thus observable as arising from want of practice, and let it restrain over-confidence resulting from theoretical knowledge alone.

The importance attached to the principles.

(3) The principles I have expounded and the hints I have imparted, deserve to be borne in mind. They are those which guide enlightened rulers. They are those which conduct them to the heights of happiness, honour and fame. They are those which alone will secure the continuance of existing independence to Native Princes.

Extension of principles of British Government to Native States.

(4) I shall conclude by quoting, in support of this position, the following valuable observation made by Her Majesty's Government so lately as in 1879. "It is in the gradual and judicious extension, in Native States, of the general principles of government which are applied in British territory that their Rulers will find the surest guarantee of their administrative independence, and the best safeguard against intervention on the part of the paramount power."

CHAPTER XXV

Fundamental Principles

April 29th 1881.

The Maharaja should become a model ruler.

We are all anxious that Your Highness should become one of the best Ruling Princes of India, that Your Highness should become a truly model Prince, an example to future Princes and a source of pride to the native community. This is the earnest wish of the great British Government which has a right to expect good government in Native States. It is likewise the wish of your numerous friends and well-wishers. It is the wish of the large body of people who are the subjects of this important State. In short, such is the universal wish.

A splendid opportunity of doing good.

(2) I feel perfectly certain that such is your own wish also. God has given you a splendid opportunity of doing public good and of achieving high honour and distinction yourself. I trust that the future History of Baroda will record the fact that Your Highness made the best possible use of that opportunity.

(3) It is not, however, enough to merely wish to become one of the best Ruling Princes of India. The mere wish cannot realise itself. You have to work for it—you have to take pains to accomplish that wish. It cannot be a difficult task to one of Your Highness' intelligence and earnestness.

The Maharaja must work.

(4) It is now my privilege and duty to lay before Your Highness a series of fundamental principles, the due observance of which will enable you to become one of the best ruling princes of India. These are great principles recognised by all good Governments. It will not be enough that you learn those principles. You must understand and digest them. Further, you must keep them constantly before you, and practically follow their guidance in every act of administration. If you simply learn those principles, but neglect to give effect to them in daily life, it would be quite as foolish as, and it would be more culpable than, a navigator possessing himself of a good mariner's compass, but not looking at it in steering his vessel.

A few principles recognised by all good Governments.

(5) Some persons of the old school might possibly say "why should the present Gaekwar learn and follow those principles? The preceding Gaekwars did not do so, and yet they managed to govern this State. The present Gaekwar may do just as they did,"

Old School objections.

The old days and the new.

(6) But let me frankly tell Your Highness that the preceding Gaekwars were hardly among the best Ruling Princes. They governed in the old arbitrary Asiatic fashion. They did not pay much regard to the happiness of the people, and, even if they did pay some regard, they did not know the best ways of promoting that happiness. Sometimes they made great errors. Occasionally they got involved in serious difficulties. Some narrowly escaped dethronement. And Your Highness well knows of the sad fate which overwhelmed Mulhar Rao. All this could have been avoided if those Gaekwars had learnt and observed right principles. The former Gaekwars, however, were not so fortunate as to have the opportunity of learning those principles as Your Highness now has. This is not all. Times and circumstances have undergone a great change. Formerly bad government in Baroda did not attract much attention, as Baroda was then an out-of-the-way place. But now-a-days Baroda has rapid railway communication with Bombay and with other important centres, both north and south. Everything that takes place in Baroda territories becomes widely and quickly known.

How mis-government might affect outsiders.

(7) Again, in consequence of railway communication, the outside people come into Baroda territories oftener and in larger numbers. And misgovern-

ment in these territories would therefore affect such people more than before and would be a matter of louder outcry.

The natural desire of the people to compare.

(8) Again, our own people have close and more frequent intercourse with Bombay and other centres. They thus have far better opportunities to compare the Government under which they live with that under which their neighbours live.

A higher ideal of government.

(9) Again, in consequence of the progress of intelligence and education, our own people have now a higher ideal of good government than before. What bad government they tolerated in past times, they would not tolerate now. What little (good) government satisfied them in past times, would not satisfy them now.

Progress with the times.

(10) Again, formerly almost all Native States were misgoverned more or less; and even British territories were in a backward condition. But now there is good progress all round, though in different degrees. The consequence is that, if we do not also fairly advance, the fact would become marked and would cause dissatisfaction.

The British Government more sensitive to misgovernment in States.

(11) And lastly, it should be noted that the British Government, as the paramount power in India, is now-a-days more sensitive to misgovernment in Native

States than before. The British Government holds itself responsible to prevent gross misgovernment in Native States. In effect, the British Government says to each Native Prince: "Formerly if you grossly maladministered your territories, a nativial remedy came into operation, namely, your subjects rose in rebellion and put an end to the tyranny. The fear of such a contingency acted as a check upon misgovernment. But now we do not and we should not permit the violent remedy of rebellion on the part of your people. We have undertaken to put down any such rebellion by employing our military force whenever necessary. We have thus deprived the people of the power of correcting tyranny. But tyranny must be corrected. Who is to correct it? We, the paramount power in India, have undertaken this duty on behalf of the people. When, therefore, the people complain of gross misgovernment in a Native State, we, the British Government, will enquire into the matter, and set it right. If found necessary we, the British Government, will even depose the misgoverning Prince and place another on the Gadi of the State."

Illustration from history.

(12) Such is the reasoning of the paramount power. It has much force and justice in it. Every Native Prince must bear in mind the fact that such is the reasoning of the great paramount power

which completely holds India from Cape Comorin to the Himalayas. The deposition of Maharaja Mulhar Rao here in Baroda itself is a recent illustration of such reasoning. History furnishes other illustrations.

Govern well.

(13) It follows, then, that the paramount power has become an important judge as to good government and bad government in the Native States. We, in Native States, must not overlook this great fact. We must constantly take care that the British Government is fairly satisfied that we are governing well—that, at least, we are not misgoverning.

Study what is good and what is bad government.

(14) Hence it further follows that we should study what the British Government would consider good, and what bad government. We should study the fundamental principles recognized by the British Government itself.

We must be more careful in these days.

(15) Your Highness will thus see how times, conditions, and circumstances have changed—how we, in our days, have to be much more careful in the work of government than former Gaekwars were. Hence the absolute necessity of this preliminary special preparation, on the part of Your Highness, for the great and responsible duties which will devolve on you before long.

The first duty of the ruler is to promote the happiness of the people.

(16) I will now proceed to lay before you some of those great fundamental principles which are essential to good government. I beg your most earnest attention to them, because I feel sure that by your being guided by those principles, you will secure for yourself the most honourable and prosperous career. The most important principle is that it is the first duty of the ruler to promote the happiness of his people. What the happiness of the people consists of, and how that happiness should be promoted, are matters which we shall consider hereafter. They are matters of extensive detail and may admit of some difference of opinion. But there can be no doubt,—there can be no divergence of opinion whatever—as to the principle itself that it is the first duty of the ruler to promote the happiness of his people.

Apply the principle constantly.

(17) Repeat this grand principle again and again. Give it the very best place in your memory. Apply it constantly to your public acts. Insist on your servants through all their gradations, from the Dewan downwards, paying the utmost respect to that principle at all times and places.

Be true to it.

(18) Be always true to that grand principle as the very foundation of your safety comfort, honour and prosperity.

The Hindu Dharma Shastras strongly prescribe that principle. It has the strongest approval of the British Government. It has the strongest approval of your people. It has the strongest recommendation of your best friends and well-wishers, among whom Mr. Elliot and myself claim a place. Many a prince while he readily enough accepts that grand principle when generally enunciated, fails to act up to it in the actual work of administration. We are all sanguine that Your Highness will not be one of such princes.

Examples contrary to this principle.

(19) The grand principle I am earnestly endeavouring to impress is, that it is the first duty of the ruler to promote the happiness of his people. A few examples of acts which would be contrary to this principle will probably strengthen the impression desired. I proceed to give a few simple examples.

(a) Diverting public funds to a selfish purpose.

(*a*) A Maharaja wishes to lay out excessive sums of money in purchasing personal jewellery, and for this purpose, makes large demands on the public treasury beyond the fair and reasonable proportion of the revenue which he may have for palace or personal expenditure. He then acts contrary to the grand fundamental principle I am trying to impress, because he diverts public funds to a selfish purpose—public funds which would otherwise have gone to promote the happiness of the people in one way or another. Let no one hastily conclude that I forbid the purchase of all jewellery by the Maharaja. The Maharaja may, of course, make purchases whenever necessary or desirable, but it must be within reasonable limits. This will be evident from a careful consideration of the words I have used in the preceding paragraph.

(b) Building Palaces.

(*b*) To proceed to another example. A Maharaja goes on building palace after palace beyond reasonable requirements, and for this purpose makes large demands on the public treasury beyond the fair and reasonable proportion of the revenue which he may have for palace or personal expenditure. He then acts contrary to the grand principle under reference. It is quite desirable that the Maharaja should have sufficient. There is a limit in this direction. The Sultan of Turkey, and the Khedive of Egypt have ruined their finances and brought themselves into serious difficulties by building an endless succession of new palaces. It would be folly of a culpable character to build costly palaces only to be whimsically abandoned for other new palaces.

(c) Cannons of gold and silver.

(*c*) I come now to another example. A Maharaja wishes to make cannons of gold and silver. This would be another instance of the violation of the grand principle of public happiness I am trying to impress; similarly when a Maharaja increases his army beyond the requirements of his country and merely for the personal pleasure of reviewing a large force.

(d) Grants to relations and favourites.

(*d*) Another example of the sort will be when the Maharaja wishes to make extravagant grants to relations, favourites etc., and to feed his extravagance, he draws from the public treasury excessive funds which would otherwise have been devoted to promote the happiness of the people. Here, too, are reasonable limits which must be respected.

(e) Religious grants.

(*e*) Even religious, charitable, and benevolent grants on the part of the Maharaja have their due limits under the principle I am advocating. Such grants must be moderate in order that the means of promoting the happiness of the people should not be crippled.

Give up the proposed expenditure if opposed to the principle.

(20) In short, whenever the Maharaja wishes to incur any considerable expenditure, he should call to mind the principle under advertence; and ask himself "Would this proposed expenditure promote the happiness of my people?" If he cannot conscientiously answer the question in the affirmative, then he must give up the proposed expenditure as opposed to the principle under advertence.

Private expenses to be borne by the Khangi.

(21) There may however, be items of expenditure which have no bearing on the happiness of the people and which the Maharaja still wishes to incur for his personal gratification. He may indulge the wish provided he incurs such expenditure from that fair portion of the public revenues which is appropriated for his personal expenses, *i.e.*, for the Khangi department.

The Raj is a public trust.

(22) No Maharaja who respects the principle under advertence will consider that he is at liberty to spend the public revenues just as he likes. The Raj is not the Maharaja's private estate but it is a public trust. He is entrusted with the public revenues under obligation to spend them for the public advantage. This must be constantly borne in mind.

Use discretion.

(23) This obligation, however, need not deprive the Maharaja of the liberty to spend as he likes within certain reasonable limits. As I have already said, the Maharaja may exercise this liberty with that fair portion of the public revenues which is appropriated for his personal expenses, *i.e.*, for the Khangi department.

Make yourself and the people happy.

(24) It will thus be seen that the Maharaja's private interests are quite reconcilable with the grand principle under advertence. The Maharaja may make

his people happy and at the same time may make himself also happy.

(25) What is to be always avoided is, the Maharaja seeking his personal gratification at the cost of the happiness of his people.

Do not sacrifice public happiness.

A few more examples contrary to the principle.

(35) I may here give a few more examples of the infraction of the grand principle under advertence.

(*a*) Want of an efficient Police.

(*a*) A Maharaja spends the public revenues in personal gratifications and cares not to maintain an adequate and efficient Police for the protection of the people. The people become unhappy from the prevalence and increase of crimes, such as murder, dacoities, robbery, etc.

(*b*) Want of Judicial Courts.

(*b*) Again, the Maharaja has no proper machinery for the administration of justice between man and man, then disputes increase and lead to crimes and violence in the country. The people become seriously unhappy.

(*c*) The ruler and the officers acting arbitrarily.

(*c*) Again, the Maharaja himself acts arbitrarily and allows his officers to act arbitrarily. They arbitrarily throw men into prison, they arbitrarily confiscate men's property, they arbitrarily put men to death. The people feel great uncertainty and alarm. They become very unhappy.

A few observations.

26) The grand principle under advertence is a warning against such courses. I proceed to offer a few further observations on the grand principle under advertence, namely that it is the first duty of the ruler to promote the happiness of his people.

No partiality to a particular class or creed.

(27) By the words "his people" I mean all his people, generally all classes and all creeds. So far as it may be possible in practice, the Maharaja should treat all classes and creeds with favour and consideration. Some classes and creeds should not be made to suffer in order to show more favour to other classes and creeds. The Maharaja should promote the happiness of all his people, whether Hindus, or Mahomedans or others, whether rich or poor, whether Sirdars, Darakdars or the common people. In short, the Maharaja should be the father—not only of any section of his people—but of all his people.

Maharaja should be the father of all his people.

(28) This is not only just and proper in itself but it is very desirable as a matter of good policy. The Maharaja who treats all his people with favour and consideration is sure to obtain the support of all his people. On the other hand, the Maharaja who treats only a section of his people with favour, will be weakened by the antagonism of the other sections. This is a very important

consideration which deserves to be remembered in the work of administration.

Employ all classes in public service.

(29) One consequence of what I have just stated is, that persons of requisite qualifications should be eligible for public employment, from all classes and creeds of the subject population in due proportion. It would be wrong to employ Deccanis only, or Gujaratis only, or Mahomedans only, or Parsis only. As already stated, all these should be employed in due proportion.

Unequal taxes to be avoided.

(30) Another consequence of what I have stated is, that no one section of the people should be burdened with taxes beyond, or in excess of other sections.

Equal justice to be dispensed to all.

(31) Another consequence of what I have stated is, that equal justice should be dispensed to all people, irrespective of class and creed. Suppose there is a suit between a Brahmin and a Mahomedan, it would be highly wrong in a Hindu ruler to show partiality to the Brahmin simply because he is a Brahmin.

No partiality to friends.

(32) It would be equally wrong in a Mahomedan ruler to show partiality to the Mahomedan simply because he is a Mahomedan. Similarly, no partiality should be shown to friends, favourites, dependents, etc. One great mark of good government is that impartial justice is rendered to all.

What a few Sirdars think.

(33) Certain persons of the Sirdar and Darakdars class have said to me (I am not sure with what degree of seriousness) that they regard the State as made for the Maharaja and for themselves ; that it is the duty of the ministers to collect the largest revenues possible and to make them available for the happiness of the Maharaja and of themselves. As for the people in general, little or no importance is attached by those persons to their (people's) happiness. Now I need not say that that is an absurdly wrong theory. It is quite opposed to all I have been saying to-day. I have no doubt that those persons will speak to Your Highness in the same way or to the same effect. Your Highness will not, of course, give any countenance to such foolish ideas. And I trust that the progress of intelligence will speedily drive out such ideas from all heads in Baroda altogether.

Their happiness not to be secured at public cost.

(34) The Sirdars and Darakdars are, of course, entitled to protection and consideration as forming a component—perhaps an important component—part of the people. But it cannot be allowed that the happiness of the Sirdars and Darakdars is to be secured at the sacrifice of that of the great body of the people.

Summary.

(35) To sum up, then :—The first duty of the Maharaja is to promote the happiness of his people—of all his people

impartially. The Maharaja who fulfills this fundamental duty to the utmost extent in his power secures the greatest attachment of his people and is, therefore, most firmly seated on his Gadi. He will have the least troubles and anxieties in the government of his country. He will secure his own personal happiness to the utmost. He will be maintained, supported and honoured most by the paramount power.

People will be happy in the ruler.

(36) The people must always have reason to say to themselves: "We are governed by a Maharaja who feels most anxious for our happiness, and who does his best with this view. Such a Maharaja is sure to teach his children to follow his own good example. We must therefore always pray for the continuance of his Dynasty."

Governments that have lived longest.

(37) History is a great magazine of experience. It will be found from this experience that, as a rule, those governments which most promoted the happiness of the people—which most respected the grand principle under advertence, lived longest, and *vice versa.*

Success of the British Indian Government.

(38) At this moment we have before our eyes a great and conspicuous example. Look at the British Government of India. With all the unavoidable disadvantages of being a foreign government,

it is really far more powerful and far more durable than any that had preceded it. Why ? Mainly because its first principle is to promote the happiness of the people as a whole. Here and there the British Government may have made errors,—may have failed in this respect—may have exposed itself to adverse criticism. Yet, on the whole, I feel, and every thoughtful man must feel, that India cannot have any other better or even an equally or nearly equally good Government. Such a feeling is one of the strongest securities for the durability of the British Government in India. So long as such feeling lasts, the British Government in India may be expected to last as it is most desirable it should. Indeed, it is not possible to assign any limit to the durability of the British Empire in India, because British principles and institutions are such that the grand principle which is our subject to-day will never be neglected or set aside. On the contrary it will be more and more effectually carried out, under an elevated sense of national duty and of national interest on the one hand, and under the pressure of popular wishes and aspirations on the other.

The value of the principle which is the foundation of good government.

(39) If, then, a vast alien empire derives so much health and strength and durability from the grand principle under advertence, Your Highness will appreciate the value of this

principle in its bearing on the State, of which you are the head. The grand principle we have been dwelling upon to-day is at the very foundation of all good government. I trust, therefore, that Your Highness will throughly accept and assimilate it. This done, we shall derive from that principle a series of other principles of the utmost value in the work of administration.

The policy of the present administration of the State.

(40) I need not inform Your Highness that the present administration of the State has been actuated by a sincere anxiety to give effect to the principle I have been this day explaining—that is to say, as far as practicable in the circumstances. Under that principle we have attempted the gradual rectification of many things. For instance, we have provided for the security of life and property by establishing a good Police. We have organized a system of judicial tribunal for deciding disputes and for punishing offenders. We have established schools and hospitals. We are going on with public works. We have abolished several bad taxes, which had been found to be excessive. We have generally abstained from putting on new or increasing old taxes with one or two exceptions which I will explain at the proper time. We have reduced such expenditure as had little or no bearing on the

happiness of the people; and we have incurred new or increased old expenditure wherever it would promote the happiness of the people. I wish Your Highness will peruse our Administration Reports in the light of the fundamental principle which I have begun to explain to Your Highness. Though there must invariably be some shortcomings, Your Highness will, I trust, find that on the whole, and as far as circumstances allow, we have acted up to those principles.

CHAPTER XXVI

FUNDAMENTAL PRINCIPLES.

Wednesday, 4th May, 1881.

The first duty of the Maharaja.

When we met here last Wednesday, we dwelt upon the fundamental principle that it is the first duty of the Maharaja to promote the happiness of his people. From this great primary principle there flow a series of other principles of great value in the work of good government. We shall notice these one after another.

Happiness of the people is of two kinds.

(2) It is easy to perceive that the happiness of the people may be divided into two parts or kinds, *viz.*, first, that which each individual of the community may obtain for himself by means of his own exertions, and secondly, that which the individual cannot obtain for himself by means of his own exertions, but which must be secured to him by the action of the Sirkar as representing the whole community.

A few examples.

(3) I will now give a few examples of each of these kinds of happiness. The following are examples of that kind of

happiness which an individual may obtain for himself by means of his own exertions, namely :—

Happiness which can be obtained by one's own exertions.

The happiness which arises from having sufficient food, clothes, etc.

That arising from having a comfortable house.

That arising from having vessels, furniture, carriages, jewels, etc., etc.

That arising from attention to personal health.

That arising from the reading of books.

That arising from the practice of virtues.

That arising from the exercise of religion.

And so on. In fact, a large, a very large part of the happiness I am speaking of, depends on the individual himself—depends on his own industry, intelligence, economy, forethought, etc.

That which cannot be so obtained.

(4) The following, on the other hand, are examples of that kind of happiness which the individual cannot obtain for himself by means of his own exertions, but which must be secured for him by the action of the Sirkar as representing the whole community, namely :—

The happiness arising from the feeling that he will not be robbed, or otherwise forcibly dispossessed of his property

—or fraudulently dispossessed of the same.

That arising from the feeling that he will not be murdered or wounded, or otherwise injured in his person.

That arising from the feeling that his disputes with others will be fairly investigated and justly decided.

That arising from the feeling that he is free to labour for his own benefit without being molested or interfered with by others.

That arising from the feeling that there are good roads and other communications available in the country for the purpose of commercial and other intercourse.

That arising from the feeling that good sanitary arrangements are enforced in cities, towns and hamlets, so that diseases and other evils are prevented as far as possible.

That arising from the feeling that good medical assistance is within reach for the cure or mitigation of diseases.

That arising from the feeling that good schools are available for the instruction of children.

And so on.

The first sort to be left to the people but the Sarkar to look to the other.

(5) The happiness of the people thus falls into two classes. First, that which each person can obtain for himself and secondly, that which each person cannot himself obtain, but which must be provided by the Sarkar. Bearing this division in mind, I proceed to say that the first mentioned class of happiness may generally be left to the people themselves, that is to say the Sarkar need not generally trouble itself about it; and the second mentioned class of happiness must be provided by the Sarkar as a matter of fundamental duty. Let us dwell further on this topic as it is of great practical importance. Be it especially noted that the Sarkar must perform the fundamental duty just mentioned, not only because it provides much happiness in itself to the people, but also because it is essential to enable the people to obtain for themselves that happiness which generally lies in their own power. In other words, if the Sarkar fail to perform that duty, it puts it largely out of the power of the people to make themselves happy by their own exertions. In other words, again, if the Sarkar fail to perform that duty, it results in the general unhappiness of the people.

Maintain a good Police.

(6) We must then recognize and remember that the most imperative duty of the Sarkar is to do that for the happiness

of the people which they cannot individually do for themselves. I proceed to give the main particulars of that great duty. The Sarkar should establish and maintain a good Police for the country in general. The object of doing so is, of course, to prevent offences as far as possible, and when, not withstanding preventive measures, offences are committed, to find out the offenders, and bring them to punishment.

The Police to be efficient.

(7) The Police force should be efficient to fulfil that object. In other words it should have a sufficient number of men and officers, in proportion to the area of the country and to the population of the same. It should be well paid as an important inducement for good behaviour. It should be selected so as to secure men and officers of intelligence, activity and integrity. It should be carefully distributed throughout the country so as to benefit every part of the same.

Rules to be laid down for their guidance.

(8) Moreover, good rules should be laid down for the guidance of the Police. What it should do and what it should not do should be clearly defined. Any misconduct on the part of the Police should be brought to light, and duly punished. Otherwise the Police would in itself become a source of oppression to the people.

(9) Bad and avaricious Native rulers fail more or less in establishing and maintaining a good Police force. Their reason is that the Police costs a large sum of money, while it yields no revenue to the Maharaja. Such Maharajas are certainly very stupid indeed. The Police is as necessary for the people as the Palace Guards are necessary for the Maharaja himself. The Police as much protects the lives, persons and property of the Maharaja and family. How stupid would it be for the ruler to say "I will have no Palace Guards because they eat up money while they do not yield any money!" It will be equally stupid for any Maharaja to say "I will have no Police for the country, because they eat up money while they do not yield any revenue.

The stupid idea that the Police costs much but yields no revenue

(10) Without proper Police, the people suffer in their lives, persons and property. Crimes are committed often and everywhere, such as murders, wounding, robberies, thefts and so forth. The people greatly suffer from such crimes. They suffer also from constant fear—anxiety—and alarm. The feeling of insecurity thus caused, while painful in itself, deters or diminishes the exertions of individuals to promote their own happiness. For instance, they become afraid to accumulate riches lest they should be robbed. They fear to travel

The Police are kept to prevent multiplicity of crimes.

lest they shoud be murdered, or wounded and robbed, and so on.

The present efficient Police ought to be maintained.

(11) In fulfilment of the fundamental duty we have been speaking of, the present Administration has established a fairly good Police. This Police has worked well and secured its objects. It costs about 7 lacs of rupees per annum. If the Palace Guards cost 50,000 rupees per annum, 7 lacs per annum are certainly not too much to protect the lives, persons and property of all your subjects throughout the country. Your Highness will thus perceive that it will be your imperative duty to fully maintain the existing Police. You may further improve it. But I trust Your Highness will never think of doing away with it, or of even reducing it.

Its efficiency not to be impaired.

(12) As the happiness of the people so very largely depends upon the maintenance of a good Police, Your Highness should at all times, be very particular to prevent its efficiency being in any way impaired. (The Police force should be mainly set apart for only Police work and should not be diverted to any other).

The tendency to misappropriate the Police.

(13) In Native States, there is a perpetual tendency to misappropriate the Police—to divert the men and officers from the service of the people to the service of private individuals. I beg Your High-

ness will be perpetually on your guard against this abuse. The abuse generally begins by some influential lady of the Palace calling for and obtaining the services of some Policemen for her private or personal use. The men soon lose all discipline. They make interest and it becomes impossible to get them back. In short, the men are really lost to the service of the people though borne on the list of the Police.

Its bad effects.

(14) One bad example leads to another. The example of the ladies comes to be followed by the gentlemen of the Palace. The example of the Palace leads to imitation by the public servants. The abuse multiplies. What is the consequence? While there is a large Police force on paper, a considerable portion is really doing private personal service. In connection with this subject, it should be remembered that every Policeman withdrawn from the public service diminishes the protection of the people. I have given one example of abuse, others may also arise, but I need not dwell longer on this part of the subject. I will only repeat to Your Highness that it will be most essential to good government that you maintain an adequate and efficient Police at all times.

They are a source of Political strength.

(15) I will now adduce another weighty consideration in favour of your maintaining an adequate and efficient Police. It is this that such Police

will be a source of political strength to yourself. There are some turbulent tribes and classes of people in these territories, easily excited or misled. They are apt to join in any movement against the Sarkar. There are past instances of their having repeatedly done so. And more intelligent intriguers are not wanting, who would make any use of those troublesome elements if there be good chance of success. Now an adequate and well distributed Police force will watch all those fellows who will be deterred from mischief from the very knowledge that they are being watched. Much mischief will thus be absolutely prevented. Again, if notwithstanding any mischief does take place, it will be observed at its very outset, and will be checked easily before it gathers force. This is of the utmost importance, for, remember this that every day a mischievous movement is left unnoticed and unchecked, it grows stronger and more extensive. The confidence of the mischief-makers increases. They compel or persuade others to join them. By looking they acquire money to support the movement. They get their followers to commit serious offences and then tell these followers "The Sarkar will never excuse you for these offences. On the contrary, if you yield, the Sarkar will punish you most severely. Your only hope of escaping punishment is to defy the Sarkar as long as you possibly can. At worst, better to die fighting against the Sarkar, than to yield and be ignominiously hanged." In this way, a small beginning might swell to great proportions. What an efficient Police could have easily put down at its incipient stage, might require an army to suppress. It may be compared to the progress of a conflagration. If the fire be noticed at the very commencement, it can be easily quenched. But the longer it is left unchecked, the more formidable it grows.

Even the British subjects may suffer for want of an efficient Police.

(16) I have not exhausted the arguments in favour of the maintenance of an efficient Police. Without an efficient Police, not only Your Highness' subjects but the subjects of the British Government will suffer. With abundant facilities for communication, British subjects come into these territories constantly and in large numbers. If British subjects are often murdered, wounded or looted in our territories in consequence of our not having an efficient Police, the British Government may take notice of the fact as evidence of mal-administration. Your Highness well knows how much it is our interest to keep the British Government fairly satisfied.

We should help the British Police.

(17) Again, it is generally our interest and duty to prevent any bodies of our people going into British territories and committing serious offences. We should prevent such things reasonably,

and if our people do commit offences in British territories and come back into ours, we should, by all means, apprehend them and make them over to the British authorities for trial and punishment. But how is all this to be done without an efficient Police ?

(18) Again, we always want the cordial assistance of the British Police in apprehending and delivering over to us those who commit serious offences in our territories and take shelter in British territories. Unless we bring such culprits to punishment, our territories will suffer terribly. But how can we expect cordial assistance from the British Police without ourselves having an efficient Police to reciprocate such assistance ?

And expect help from them in return.

(19) What I have said in regard to British territories, more or less applies also to other neighbouring territories. I think I have said enough to strongly impress on Your Highness the vital importance of maintaining an adequate and efficient Police for the protection of the people. Such Police has been already established. It is now working so well, that our territories can stand honourable comparison with neighbouring British territories in respect to public peace, order and security; whereas a few years ago, the Baroda territory was very badly off in these

Our territories to stand honorable comparison with other territories.

respects. What you have then to do is to maintain the Police we thus already have. Let nothing whatever induce you to impair that Police. You can, of course, further improve it.

Worthless opinions of certain persons.

(20) Certain persons here, (and I am glad they are very few,) will probably tell you that the present administration has done wrong in establishing this Police force, and thereby adding to the public expenditure. When any person tells you so, my advice is, quietly take out Your Highness' notebook and mark him as a person whose opinion is worthless in public affairs. As bearing on the subject under consideration, let us read paras, 82, 83 and 84 of our Administration Report for the year 1878-79, page 52. (Here read and explain the same). There are also other paras, of the same Administration Report which may be read and explained with interest in connection with the subject under treatment. Let us turn to paras. 98 to 106, inclusive, page 55. (Here read and explain the same.)

The Sirdars to have nothing to do with the Police.

(21) It follows that, as a rule, the Sirdars, and Silledars should have nothing to do with the Police so long as the difficulties just explained continue. I assure Your Highness that it is much better that the Sirdars and Silledars should go on as they have been going on, than that they should

be forced into the Police so as to impair its discipline and efficiency and to bring themselves into trouble. In short, no desire for economy no wish to utilize the Sirdars and Silledars, no anxiety to meet their wishes, should be allowed for a moment, to interfere with the satisfactory performance of the fundamental duty of the Sarkar, to protect the life, person and property of the people by the maintenance of an adequate and efficient Police.

The primary duty emphasised.

(22) The Hindu Dharma-Shastras repeatedly and most strongly enjoin this primary duty on kings. I must conclude this day's lecture by declaring that he who fails to discharge this great duty is not worthy of the position, or even the name of a ruler.

CHAPTER XXVII

Fundamental Principles

11*th May*, 1881.

We began by laying down the great and fundamental principle that it is the first duty of the ruler to promote the happiness of the people. We derived from that principle the foremost obligation of all governments to take measures with the view of protecting the life, person and property of the people.

The obligation of all Governments.

2. We have seen that the first of these measures is to establish and maintain an adequate and efficient Police for the whole country.

An efficient Police.

(3) Now, the Police acts in two ways. First, it prevents offences as far as may be possible. Secondly, when offences are committed in spite of preventive efforts, the great duty of the Police is to catch the offenders and to bring them to punishment.

The two-fold functions of the Police.

(4) In both these respects the Police has, or may have, to use force—mainly physical force. It has to use force to overcome the force with which it

The Police represents the ordinary physical force of the ruler.

may be opposed. Offenders cannot be expected to quietly obey orders or to surrender themselves without resistance. The Police should be strong enough to overcome the ordinary resistance which it may encounter. It is evident, then, that the Police represents the ordinary physical force of the ruler. A ruler without a Police is like a man without muscular power. He may talk, write, issue orders ever so wisely, but he will not be able to act; —he will not be able to compel obedience.

But a superior force is necessary.

(5) I have said that the Police represents the ordinary physical or muscular power of the ruler—that is of the State. But this is not sufficient for all contingencies. Sometimes, though not ordinarily, it may appear that many offenders combine and offer such a degree of resistance that the Police is not strong enough to put down such resistance. For example, the Police proceed to catch a Bheel murderer, hundreds of Bheels turn out to aid the offender, and to prevent the Police catching him. Suppose the assembled Bheels are so strong in numbers and deadly weapons, that the Police on the spot is unable to put them down even with the assistance of the neighbouring Police. Take another example. Some excitement or quarrel arises between a body of Hindus and a body of Mahomedans, and they proceed to attack each other in numbers. Take a third example. Some

time ago, a dispute arose between the Parsees and the Mahomedans of our town of Nowsari in regard to the route which the Taboot procession should take. I investigated the matter and decided that the Mahomedans should be allowed to take the route which has been customary for many years. The Parsees did not like my decision, but they had to submit to it, and I am glad to say that they did submit to it with that good sense which distinguishes that class of people. But suppose that the Parsees had been so foolish as to refuse to submit to the Sarkar's order—so foolish as to oppose the carrying out of the Sarkar's order. Suppose that large numbers of the Parsees assembled and, with arms in their hands resolved to resist the progress of the Taboot procession passing as directed by the Sarkar. When such contingencies arise, when the Police is not strong enough to overcome the extraordinary resistance offered,—the Sarkar must not stand still. Once allow such unlawful resistance to prevail—once allow the Sarkar's authority to be set aside or defied,—such resistance will be repeated and will be repeated until the Sarkar's authority is destroyed and anarchy ensues.

The Military force and its necessity.

(6) It being so necessary to enforce the authority of the Sarkar—so necessary to compel the resisting people to submit to the just orders of the Sarkar—we must supply some physical force far superior

to that of the ordinary Police. I allude to the Military force. Hence the necessity of a sufficient Military force for the use of the State on such occasions. The State, then must maintain a Military force. It is a duty which should be fully attended to in the interest of peace, order and security.

The Police and the Military form the whole muscular force.

(7) The Police represents the ordinary muscular power of the Sarkar. The Police and the Military together constitute the whole muscular power of the Sarkar. With this whole muscular power in good condition, the Sarkar is able to obtain obedience to its orders which it has to execute for the good of the people, for promoting the happiness of the people.

The degree of efficiency of the Military force.

(8) Let me now lay before you some of the more important points in relation to the Military force of the State. It is self-evident that the Military force should be efficient to the requisite degree. Let us now consider what this degree of efficiency is. The degree of this efficiency must be determined by references to the purposes which the Military force is required to accomplish.

It should be more efficient than the Police.

(9) I have already stated that the Military force is to be called into play when the Police is not strong enough to put down resistance. It follows then as a matter of course, that the Military force should

be more efficient than the Police. In other words, a Military department of 100 men should be more efficient than an equal Police department. We thus have the inferior or lower limit of efficiency. The limit to start from is quite clear.

It need not be as efficient as the British force.

(10) On the other hand, it should be remembered that our Military force has no occasion to fight with Afghans, Russians, etc., as British Regiments have or may have to do. It follows, then, as a matter of course, our Military force need not be as efficient as the British forces. We thus have the superior or higher limit of efficiency. The degree of efficiency of our Military force must then be somewhere above the efficiency of our Police and below the efficiency of British Regiments. Provided we keep fairly within these broad and clear lines, any little error in the fixation of the exact degree may not be of much consequence.

The present efficiency is sufficient.

(11) I may here inform Your Highness that I consider that the present efficiency in which our regular force is maintained is generally sufficient for our purposes. Your Highness will, therefore, have to maintain that degree of efficiency.

The irregulars are of no use.

(12) From what I have above explained, Your Highness will readily perceive that our irregular forces, (by which I mean the old Silledari horse and

foot) are of little or no use for the purposes in view because they do not fulfil the important condition already noted as regards efficiency. They are even much less efficient than the present ordinary Police. In short, the Silledari is an old, rusty and almost useless weapon.

Do not raise the efficiency of the regular force.

(13) Another conclusion following from what I have said is that Your Highness will do well to firmly resist the temptation to raise the efficiency of our regular force to the British standard. Such temptation may arise from a mere personal love of display or from hasty and thoughtless recommendations made by our own; or even by British Officers. Military Officers have a natural and excusable wish to raise the quality of their forces to the highest possible standard without much regard for the necessities of the case, or for the expenditure involved.

But the present efficiency to be maintained.

(14) On the other hand, it will be necessary to take care that the present efficiency does not fall off. In Native States, laxity is very apt to creep in in consequence of neglect or indifference. There is need to be vigilant against such a tendency.

The usefulness of this physical power.

(15) I think it will be useful here to peruse the observations made in the Administration Report for 1878-79 under the head of Military department. The sum

and substance of what I have been urging is that the present Regular Military force should be maintained in its existing Police, both representing the physical power of the Sarkar, a power absolutely necessary for the proper performance of the Sarkar's fundamental duty of protecting the life, person and property of the subjects. With this physical power at the command of the Sarkar, the Sarkar will be able to enforce obedience to its orders whether these orders are in the shape of laws or those which are issued from time to time.

Another requisite is a proper machinery for the administration of justice.

(16) To proceed. The protection of the life, person and property of the people requires something more than a Police force plus a Military force. An equally essential requisite is a proper machinery for the administration of justice. By a proper machinery for the administration of justice, I mean courts—such as that of the magistrate, that of the munsiff, that of the zilla judge, and that of the Varisht Judge—a series of courts with graduated powers, for administering civil and criminal justice, the duty of these courts being to decide justly all the numerous disputes which constantly arise among the people themselves.

To settle the innumerable differences and disputes.

(17) The people are, of course, a body of individuals. Differences and disputes constantly arise between individual and individual. If these differences

and disputes are not justly investigated and decided as they arise, see what grave evils will ensue. Individual will fight with individual, family with family, bodies of persons with other bodies. Small matters will grow into large matters. Strong passions will be excited. Breaches of the peace will constantly occur. Killing, wounding, plundering will become very common. The motives for peaceful, steady industry will be greatly weakened—perhaps extinguished. The motives for the accumulation of wealth will similarly suffer. In short, great confusion will prevail and the happiness of the people will be destroyed.

Courts of justice to be established.

(18) But we started with the fundamental principle that it is the first duty of the ruler to promote the happiness of the people. Of what use that ruler be, who allows the happiness of the people to be destroyed in the manner I have just stated? It will thus be seen how essential it is for good government to establish courts of justice. Maintaining good courts of justice, the Sarkar says to the people, " Don't you quarrel and fight among yourselves. Whenever any individual feels he has been injured by another in respect of person, or property, or otherwise, let the complainant represent the matter to the judicial tribunals, and these tribunals will carefully enquire into the matter and decide the dispute justly. The wrong-doer

will be found out, he will be compelled to make reparation for the wrong he has done, and when such is necessary, he will be also punished for the wrong he did."

Wrong-doers are restrained by the fear of courts.

(19) The great body of the people like such an arrangement. The very existence of the arrangement largely prevents many wrongs and many disputes. Each individual says to himself "I must not do any wrong to my neighbour or take from him what is justly his; for, as soon as I do so, I will be deprived of my gain, and I may be also punished." Many people will reason in this way and abstain from wrong-doing. This, Your Highness, is an immense and incalculable benefit to society. To realise this benefit adequately, you must think over the matter. Meanwhile let me assure you—and on reflection you will thoroughly understand it—that the great body of the people who do not actually use the judicial machinery (*i. e.*, the courts) really benefit by that machinery much more than those comparatively few people who do use that machinery. Why is it that the great body of the people do not resort to the courts? Because they have not been wronged. But why have they not been wronged? Because wrong-doers have been restrained by the fear of the courts. To make the matter clearer, let us take some figures merely by way of example. Our subjects

are, say, 20 lakhs. Out of this, suppose half a lakh have recourse to the courts. Then I wish to explain to Your Highness that this half a lakh derive much benefit, because they obtain redress for their grievances, but the rest of the people—19½ lakhs—benefit still more because they have been successfully protected against injuries—protected in consequence of the very existence of the courts.

The whole population is benefitted.

(20) Your Highness will thus see that the courts are of great benefit to the whole population—that the courts constitute one of the most effective instruments for the protection of life, person and property—a protection which we have recognised to be the fundamental duty of the Ruler.

Peace and order prevail, and the people's happiness promoted.

(21) It is owing to the operation of the judicial tribunals that the weak are protected against the strong—the good are protected against the bad. It is owing to the operation of the judicial tribunal that peace and order prevail, and that men are enabled to enjoy as much liberty as possible, and are enabled to exert themselves for their happiness without being molested by others. It is owing to the operation of the judicial tribunals that society is kept well together; that the forces which tend to promote the happiness of society have free action, and that those forces are prevented from acting against each other and consequently neutralising

or weakening each other. All the forces tending to promote the happiness of society being thus directed in one channel, the greatest and best results are secured. Take any two States equal in all other respects, but the one having a good judicial machinery and the other having a bad judicial machinery or none. It is quite certain that, that State which has a good judicial machinery will prosper beyond the other in a very decided manner. We thus see how essential and valuable the administration of justice is to accomplish the great object of government, namely, the happiness of the people.

The existing judicial machinery must be maintained.

(22) Now we have succeeded in establishing in these territories a series of judicial tribunals, such as the country requires. These judicial tribunals have been working well and are fulfilling their objects. If all that I have been this day saying has made a sufficient impression on Your Highness (and I need not doubt it), I feel sure that Your Highness will earnestly maintain and support the existing judicial machinery. A contrary course would be ruinous alike to the people and to the ruler. I feel quite certain of this; and pray remember one additional circumstance, that when a community has already known and felt the advantage of a good administration of justice, the mischief and the peril of depriving that community of a good administration of justice would be all the greater.

The Maharaja cannot do judicial work personally.

(23) In connection with the administration of justice, I wish Your Highness to realise the fact that, in any large State, it would be utterly impossible for the Maharaja to himself personally do regular judicial work. It would be too burdensome to the Maharaja, and it is not possible for every Maharaja to qualify himself with the necessary amount of legal knowledge and experience, to acquire which years of study are required—perhaps a good portion of a life-time. It follows that there should be a regularly constituted judicial machinery, such as at present exists—a machinery which will work steadily from day to day without necessitating the Maharaja personally taking trouble. It would be wrong—it would be contrary to the interests of the people—to delay justice because the Maharaja is engaged in ceremonies, or festivities, or tired of work, or feels indisposed in point of health or for such other reasons.

If he undertakes it, he must fail.

(24) Let me inform Your Highness of the clear result of my study and experience, namely, that any Maharaja who undertakes to administer public justice personally must inevitably fail.

Trained judges should dispense public justice.

(25) There are yet other strong reasons in support of the maintenance of the existing judicial machinery. I must lay them before Your Highness.

Judges who have made law and justice their special study, who hold office on the express condition of dispensing justice—who are constantly alive to their responsibility—who are under fear of discredit and disgrace consequent on misdecision—I say that judges will generally deserve and command far greater confidence as dispensers of public justice than even the Maharaja, himself. This will be quite evident on reflection. It being so, it is for the best interests of the people that trained and constituted judges should dispense public justice, and not that the Maharaja should undertake the task personally. I must frankly tell Your Highness that if I had a suit of any importance, I would consider it better and safer that the judges should decide the case than that the Maharaja should do so, even though the Maharaja is a well-educated ruler. It is just like this, namely that, in case of serious illness, I would decidedly prefer to be treated by a trained doctor to being treated by the Maharaja. Again, I would decidedly prefer that the railway train in which I am to travel, be driven by the trained driver, to its being driven by an amateur Maharaja. Your Highness will find that those few who would prefer the Maharaja as a judge are very few indeed—a mere drop in the ocean. And the preference shown by those few persons clearly arises, not from a wish to obtain pure justice, but from the wish to obtain decisions in their favour under the very objectionable system of *Meherbani.*

Why the Maharaja should not dispense justice personally.

(26). Again. If the Maharaja were to dispense justice personally, he would be sure, in a few years, to incur the enmity or ill-will of great numbers of the people ; for, he must inevitably displease all those against whom he ever decides. It is difficult to set limits to the possible consequences of that enmity or ill-will. I need not be more explicit. Why should the Maharaja expose himself to such enmity or ill-will ? It is quite needless. It would certainly be very unwise in any Maharaja to place himself in such a position.

The parties are sure to appeal.

(27) Again. The dissatisfied parties are sure to appeal to the Agent, Governor-General. They may appeal to the Viceroy. They may appeal to the public through the newspapers. Now, if the Maharaja were to personally administer justice, all those appeals would be directed against the Maharaja personally. All the appeals would go to question the Maharaja's legal knowledge, to question his impartiality, to question his care and diligence. Harsh words would be applied to the Maharaja, such as ignorance, partiality, carelessness and many other worse things. Would this be pleasant to the Maharaja ? Would it be consistent with his dignity ? Would it be consistent

with that high respect and veneration in which it is desirable the Maharaja should be held ? When the Maharaja's name is roughly handled as just indicated, the Maharaja might be tempted to resent the same. The resentment might take very unjustifiable forms amd might bring the Maharaja into more or less serious difficulties. Why incur all this risk ?

It wouldlook bad to have his decision reversed.

(28) Let us pursue the subject a little further. Suppose some of the appeals result in the conclusion that the Maharaja's decision appealed against was wrong, and must therefore be reversed. What would be the consequence ? Why, the Maharaja would surely feel a degree of humiliation which would be very painful to him, which would probably deprive him of his sleep and digestion for some time. This would be the case especially when the Maharaja is compelled to cancel his own decision with his own hand and to pass a fresh order in favour of the party against whom he has decided—the very party who had probably abused the Maharaja in the appeal. In such a situation, how would the Maharaja look in the eyes of his people ?

Bribery is sure to creep in.

(29) Again, if the Maharaja administers justice personally, he would be more or less assisted in the work by certain karkoons or other officials around him. As the parties themselves cannot have free access to

the Maharaja, those officials would be likely to be openly or secretly engaged by the parties to make representations or explanations in their behalf to the Maharaja. Bribery is pretty sure to creep in and take root. Defeated parties will attribute their defeat, not to the weakness of their cause, but to bribes paid by the opposite party. Charges of corruption, true or false, will be prepared. Investigation of such charges cannot be refused, as a rule. Prosecutions will have to be ordered. Such prosecutions may involve not only the officials about the Maharaja, but even higher persons,—perhaps friends, relations, Mankaries. etc. All this would be unpleasant in the highest degree, especially when convictions and punishments follow.

The British Government watches the kind of justice imparted.

(30) The administration of justice has, in these days, become a matter of far greater difficulty than ever before. The concerns of the people have become more complicated. The demand for justice on the part of the people is more exacting. And, in consequence of railways, etc., many British and other outside people come under our justice. It is to be always remembered that the British Government watches to see what kind of justice its subjects get in Native States. This is another important reason why the Maharaja should not burden himself with judicial work.

(31) Your Highness will thus see what weighty reasons there are for maintaining the existing judicial machinery and for giving it your hearty support. We now enjoy a high reputation in respect of the administration of justice. It is a source of immense strength to us. May Your Highness always enjoy this strength.

The high reputation of the administration.

(32) In Native States, I am ashamed to say, the administration of justice is not much looked after, because it does not bring in revenue largely; and what revenue it may bring in, is hardly sufficient to pay the judicial machinery. I do not say this of all Native States, for there are exceptional instances of some States maintaining a very fair system of judicial administration. But a Maharaja, who knows what his great and fundamental duties are, will never fail to maintain a good judicial administration essential for the happiness and prosperity of his people.

In other states the administration of justice not properly looked after.

(33) I cannot too strongly impress on Your Highness the prime necessity of maintaining a pure administration of justice. Without it, human beings, with their various feelings and passions, cannot long live together and prosper in their concerns. Cost what they may, the existing courts of

The courts pay a portion of their cost by fees and fines.

justice must be maintained. But they pay a good portion of their cost by means of fees and fines.

The special court for suits against Sirdars.

(34) Among the existing courts, Your Highness knows that there is a special court for suits against Sirdars. This special court has been designed to conciliate the feelings and sentiments of this class of people who do not wish to be subject to the ordinary courts. As long as these feelings and sentiments prevail, this special and distinct court of justice must be maintained. The great principle to be remembered in this respect is, that the Sirdars cannot for a moment be allowed to claim to be beyond the reach of public justice. They cannot be allowed—no human being can be allowed—not even the Maharaja himself—to say "we shall do any unjust things we like." This is so self-evident that no arguments are necessary. Do anything and everything that may be reasonable to gratify the Sirdars, in respect of their peculiar feelings of dignity, etc., but it must be all consistent with the great principle that they must be substantially subject to public justice, like other members of the community.

Maintain a proper and self-working judicial machinery.

(35) The particulars as to the constitution, the powers, and the functions of the various tribunals of justice fall within the province of Mr. Cursetji to explain to Your Highness. But in expounding

fundamental principles of good government, my duty is to impress on Your Highness the absolute necessity of maintaining a proper and permanent and self-working judicial machinery. As your sincere well-wisher, as a faithful and experienced public servant, I assure you that the maintenance of an efficient judicial machinery is quite essential to the stability of your power as a ruler.

The abominable system of nazaranas to get favourable decisions.

(36) In connection with the administration of justice, I must here allude to the abominable system of nazaranas which prevailed here. In fact, the parties to a suit freely offered money to the Maharaja to get decisions in their favour. That party who made the largest gift of money generally got the decision in his favour. This was really selling justice to the highest bidder. This is the worst kind of avarice that any ruler can be guilty of. A ruler making money by selling justice is worse than that despicable man who makes money by selling his own children. I earnestly hope that the nazarana system I am speaking of has received its death-blow, and it will never more raise its horrid head again.

Bribery should receive its death blow.

(37) It will not, however, be enough for the ruler himself to abstain from taking nazarana or bribesin connection with the administration of justice. He must be always vigilant to prevent his friends,

relations, dependents, etc., from doing the same directly or indirectly—openly or secretly. There are lots of hungry wolves infesting Palaces, though they appear like lambs ; and the Baroda Palace is not an exception. I know that even among those who are well off,and who are outwardly respectable and gentlemanly, there are some quite ready to take bribes without caring anything for the good name of the Maharaja, and for the welfare of the people. Against such rogues, Your Highness should be perpetually on your guard. When, therefore, Your Highness assumes power, you must unmistakably make it known to all around you that, if any one takes bribes, he will have no mercy, but that he will be turned out of the Palace by you ; that he will lose his nemnooks and privileges ; and that he may be prosecuted in due course of justice and adequately punished. If, notwithstanding such previous and particular warning, any one misbehaves, lethim certainly feel Your Highness' displeasure, more or less, in the manner above stated ; and one or two practical examples will surely stop the evil. The exposure and punishment of a possible friend, relation or dependent may be very unpleasant ; but it is an imperative duty which you owe as a ruler to your subjects. If the fellow did not care about your reputation, you need not care about his. In relation to this subject, let us always remember that it was bribery and corruption which mainly brought about the downfall of Mulhar Rao.

The officers to be of good character.

(38) I have stated and repeated that a pure administration of justice is essential to the well-being of the people. To make sure of such an administration of justice, other conditions are also required and let us notice the chief of them. It is very important that the officers appointed to administer justice should be men of good character and possessing the requisite knowledge of judicial work. In fact, there can be no good government without men of honesty and qualification to work in all the main departments of government. How such men should be sought out and availed of, is in itself a very important subject, which I shall treat of separately hereafter. I will here only say that magistrates, munsiffs and judges should be very carefully selected persons. Above all, the judges of the Varishta, or your highest court, should be the very best men possible. This advantage secured, all the rest will follow easily enough.

They must be well paid.

(39) The judicial officers—(indeed all officers) must be well paid. Of this subject, also, I will speak hereafter in a distinct lecture.

And promoted according to merit.

(40) The judicial officers—(indeed all officers)—must be generally promoted according to merit and good public service.

(41) The judicial officers especially should have confidence in the tenure of their offices, so long as they behave well, and have health and strength for work. They must not be afraid of being removed arbitrarily. Above all, they should have no reason to fear that they might be injured, because of the displeasure that they might incur by doing impartial justice.

Should not be removed arbitrarily.

(42) The Maharaja should scrupulously abstain from asking the judicial officers to decide this way or that way in particular cases. The Maharaja should not even show that he would be pleased if any particular party be favoured. He should show no special interest on either side. His attitude should clearly indicate that he cares only for the impartial administration of justice, and that he will strongly support every judicial officer who distributes justice without fear or favour. To maintain this attitude, the Maharaja will have to resist importunities of friends, relations and dependents, with great firmness. These should be once for all ordered not to trouble Your Highness in that manner. If, notwithstanding, any one does trouble Your Highness, Your Highness' reply should be "I cannot influence the judicial officers in any way. I have appointed good judges and they will do justice. If you are not satisfied with the

The administration should be impartial.

decision, you may appeal to the higher court. In this way, you can obtain what justice you may be entitled to." Some such reply, firmly repeated, will effectually check importunity. Otherwise, that is to say, if you yield to importunity in a few instances—importunity will increase and multiply; you would be perpetually worried every moment of your life, and the administration of justice will go wrong—your reputation as a good ruler will suffer.

No special relaxation, in favour of Palace servants.

(43) Again. The Maharaja will do well to show his respect for justice by supporting the courts when they require the attendance of Palace servants and officials. All requisitions which are right and proper should be readily complied with. Those servants and officials should be made to feel that they are not above justice—that they are responsible to justice—that they must respect others' rights—just like other subjects. They should feel that no special relaxation of justice will take place in their favour, though they will be well protected as long as they behave well. They are all generally shrewd people who will be anxious to study the disposition of the Maharaja and to submit to the same.

Refer all civil and criminal matters to the courts.

(44) The Maharaja should personally set a good example to all by his own habitual and cordial respect for justice. For instance, the Maharaja

should abstain from using or causing any personal violence to—from inflicting any personal ill-treatment on any of his servants. His Highness should abstain from himself ordering arbitrary imprisonment, attachment, or confiscation of property, etc., etc. His Highness should refer all offences and civil disputes to his courts, who will do the needful in the proper way. Again, His Highness should readily pay all the monies due by him to others. He must satisfy all just claims just like any private individual. He should satisfy such claims, as far as possible, without compelling the claimants to abandon their claims or to resort to the courts of justice. Such a course on the part of His Highness will save him much personal enmity and will promote his popularity while strengthening the cause of justice generally.

But see that the courts fulfil their duties.

(45) From what I have said it is not to be supposed that His Highness has nothing whatever to do with the courts of justice—that His Highness is simply to look on as an indifferent or unconcerned spectator—that His Highness is simply to let the courts do what they like. No. It is the great and imperative right and duty of His Highness not only to maintain the judicial machinery, but to see that this machinery properly fulfils its purposes. I shall take another opportunity of explaining how this is to be done. In fact, I pro-

pose to explain how this is to be done in the instance of each department of the administration, so that Your Highness may have a complete and comprehensive view of this important subject.

The Maharaja should perform sovereign duties.

(46) The great thing is that the Maharaja should be able to distinguish his own high and superintending duties from less important and mere ministerial duties. The Maharaja's ambition should be to perform sovereign duties and not the subordinate duties of officers and karkoons. It is only that Maharaja who is ignorant of sovereign duties, or who is incompetent to perform sovereign duties, it is only such a Maharaja, I say, that abandons sovereign duties and wastes his time and energies in doing lower duties which officers and karkoons would do much better, more steadily and more accurately.

Lessons from the writings of Fenelon.

(47) I will conclude this day's lecture by inviting Your Highness' best attention and study to two eloquent passages in which a great Frenchman of the name of Fenelon conveyed to his royal pupil lessons similar to those which I have been endeavouring to convey to yourself. I will leave Mr. Elliot to tell Your Highness all about that great Frenchman, but I am here chiefly concerned with the leading ideas which he

inculcated—ideas which strongly confirm what I have already said, whether particularly as regards the whole administration of justice, or generally as regards the whole administration of the Raj. The following are the two passages I allude to :—

Telemachus, P. 400.
Decide new questions of right but not of private property.

" Idomenes then complained of the perplexity he suffered from the great number of causes between private persons, which he was pressed, with great importunity, to decide. 'Decide' said Mentor, 'all new questions of right, by which some general maxim of jurisprudence will be established or some precedents given for the explanation of law already in force, but do not take upon you to determine all questions of private property; they would overwhelm and embarrass you by their variety and number. Justice would necessarily be delayed for your single decision, and all subordinate Magistrates would become useless. You would be overwhelmed and confounded, the regulations of petty affairs would leave you neither time nor thought for business of importance ; and, after all, petty affairs would not be regulated. Avoid, therefore, a state of such disadvantage and perplexity ; refer private disputes to subordinate Judges, and do nothing yourself but what others cannot do for you. You then, and then only, fulfil the duties of a king.' * * * * * "

Telemachus, P. 390-392.

To do every thing yourself is a poor ambition. To form great designs, all must be freedom and tranquillity. Government requires a certain harmony like music and just proportions like architecture.

"The proof of abilities in a king as the supreme governor of others, does not consist in doing everything himself; to attempt it is a poor ambition, and to suppose that others will believe it can be done, an idle hope. In government the king should not be the body, but the soul; by his influence and under his direction the hands should operate and the feet should walk; he should conceive what is to be done, but he should appoint others to do it. His abilities will appear in the conception of his designs and the choice of his instruments. He should never stoop to their functions, nor suffer them to aspire to his; neither should he trust them implicitly; he ought to examine their proceedings and be equally able to detect a want of judgment or integrity. He governs well who discerns the various characters and abilities of men, and employs them to administer government under him in departments that are exactly suited to their talents. The perfection of supreme government consists in the governing of those that govern; he that presides, should try, restrain and correct them; he should encourage, raise, change and displace them; he should keep them for ever in his eye and in his hand; but to make the minute particulars of their subordinate departments objects of personal application, indicates meanness and suspicion, and fills the mind with petty anxieties that leave it neither time nor liberty for designs that are worthy of royal attention. To form great designs, all must be freedom and tranquillity. No intricacies of business must embarrass or perplex, no subordinate objects must divide the attention. A mind that is enchanted upon minute particulars, resembles the lees of wine that have neither flavour nor strength; and a king who busies himself in doing the duties of his servants, is always deterred by the present appearances and never extends his view to futurity; he is always absorbed by the business of the day that is passing over him and, this being his only object, acquires an undue importance, which, if compared with others, it would lose. The mind that admits but one object at a time, must naturally contract; and it is impossible to judge well of any affair without considering many, comparing them with each other, and ranging them in a certain order by which their relative importance will appear. He that neglects this rule in government resembles a musician who should content himself with the discovery of melodious tones, one by one, and never think of combining or harmonising them into music which would not only gratify the ear, but affect the heart; or he may be compared to an architect, who should fancy the powers of his art exhausted by heaping together large columns and great quantities of stone curiously carved, without considering the proportion of his building, or the arrangement of his ornaments; such an artist, when he was building a saloon, would not reflect that a suitable staircase should be added, and when he was busy upon the body of the building, he would forget the courtyard and the portal; his work would be nothing more than a confused assemblage of parts, not suited to each other, nor concurring to form a whole; such a work would be so far from doing him honour, that it would be a perpetual monument of disgrace; it would show that his range of thought was not sufficient to include all the parts of his design at once; that his mind was contracted and his genius subordinate; for he that sees only from part to part, is fit only to execute the designs of another. Be assured, my dear Telemachus, that the government of a kingdom requires a certain harmony like music and just proportions like architecture. If you will give me leave to carry on the parallel between these arts and government, I can easily make you comprehend the inferiority of those who administer government by parts and not as a whole. He that sings particular parts in a concert, however great his skill or excellent his voice, is still but a singer; he who regulates all the parts and conducts the whole is the master of music; so he that fashions the columns and carries up the side of a building, is no more than a mason; but he who has designed the whole and whose mind sees all the relations of part to part, is the architect. Those, therefore, who are most busy, who despatch the greatest number of affairs, can least be said to govern; they are inferior workmen; the presiding mind, the genius that governs the State, is he who, doing nothing, causes all to be done; who meditates and contrives, who looks forward to the future, and back to the past, who sees relative proportions, arranges all things in order, and provides for remote contingencies. * * *"

CHAPTER XXVIII

Fundamental Principles.—(*contd.*)

1*st June* 1881.

Summary of the previous chapter.

We began by stating that it is the first duty of the ruler to promote the happiness of his people. In order to promote the happiness of the people, the first thing which the ruler has to do is to take measures for the security of the life, liberty, person and property of the people. The first of these measures is to establish and maintain an adequate and efficient Police backed by a Military force of sufficient strength and discipline, the Police and the Military bodies representing the physical or the muscular force of the Sarkar—the force by which the Sarkar is to compel obedience to law. The next immediate measure is to establish and maintain proper judicial tribunals for dispensing justice to the people; for deciding their various disputes as they arise, granting redress to injured parties and punishing offenders whenever it is desirable to do so.

(2) We have dwelt on the importance of the proper administration of justice, but for this purpose it is obviously essential that the judicial tribunals should have proper instructions from the State. It is evident that the several Judges and Magistrates cannot be left to dispense justice just as they like. They ought to have principles and rules given them by the State for their guidance. These principles and rules are known as the laws of the country.

The judicial tribunals to have proper instructions from the State.

(3) The State, then, must lay down laws for the guidance of the Judges. These laws, are in fact, the well-considered orders of the State, once for all issued for the information and guidance of the Judges, and also of the people in general. These standing or permanent orders of the State, known as laws, must be good, that is to say, the laws must be calculated to promote the happiness of the people. The happiness of the people ought to be the chief and ultimate aim of the laws.

Good laws to be laid down for their guidance.

(4) It is certainly one of the most difficult of human labours to frame a complete body of good laws for any community. Transactions between man and man are extremely numerous and sometimes very complex. Again, it requires very long experience and careful observation to determine the

Goods law are the product of long experience.

effect of any particular transaction or of any set of transactions on the general happiness of the community. Good laws must, therefore, be the product of long experience, careful observation and intellectual labours of the highest order.

In preparing laws, note the common principles of justice, known to the civilised world.

(5) We, here in Baroda, cannot pretend to evolve from our own brains all the laws which are required for the regulation of the affairs of our people. To do so would be impossible, undesirable and, after all, unnecessary. No community ever does so. One example may be adduced here to make more clear what I have just said. Suppose we wish to cure sickness among our people; there are thousands of forms of sickness and some of the most complex character. Surely, we are not to set aside the accumulated knowledge and experience of the world in general, and of similar countries in particular. We are not to set aside all that and to study all those forms of sickness ourselves and to devise our own medicines so with respect to civil and criminal laws. What should we then do with respect to laws? I will briefly answer. We should note what few laws we already have. We should carefully note the great and universal principles of justice known to the civilized world as axioms or common principles. We should also note the laws which govern similar neighbouring communities. We should

further note the good customs which have prevailed in these territories. On a combined consideration of all these, we must frame our instructions to our judicial tribunals.

(6) This is exactly the course which has been actually followed by the present administration. Indeed, any better course is not to be practically found at the beginning. It was not possible to start with a complete code of laws of our own. A work of many years cannot be done in such a comparatively short time.

It is the course followed by the present administration.

(7) Our higher judges are all men who have more or less studied law as a science. They are conversant with the great and universal principles of justice. These principles enable them to keep within the broad path of justice and to avoid any gross deviations. These principles are great safeguards in this way, and their guidance is all the more necessary at a time when we have no complete and specific code of laws of our own, when so much has therefore to be left to the discretion of the courts.

The guidance of our higher judges is necessary.

(8) Again, our community is not different from the neighbouring community under British rule. If there be any difference, it is not considerable. It may therefore, be presumed that the laws framed by the British Government for the neighbouring

Apply the laws framed by the British Government.

community, and which have been found to work well, are generally applicable to our community also. And it is to be remembered in this connection that the laws of the British Government are framed by eminently able and experienced men. Our judges know these laws or have access to them. They may well follow the spirit of these laws in the absence of anything better to guide them.

Local customs to be respected.

(9) Again, there are long-established local customs—customs recognised and acted upon by our own people. Our judges respect such customs as a most important condition of the administration of justice.

The Hindu and Muhammadan Laws, and other customs.

(10) Again, we have got authoritative works on Hindu and Muhammadan Law regulating marriage, adoption, succession to property, partition of property, etc., etc. These works are guides to our judges as much as to British Indian Judges. Customs which are not mentioned in these works, but which may still be found to exist in particular places or in particular classes of people, are also the guides of our judges who specially ascertain such customs from time to time. Under such combined guidance, our judges are enabled to render substantial justice to our people in a manner far more satisfactory than at any time before in the history of the Baroda State. And it is to be added that our Judges render substantial

justice without that, without those technicalities and elaborate forms which are a matter of complaint elsewhere.

But there is ample room for improvement.

(11) In this way we have done the best that has been possible in the circumstances of the situation for the administration of justice. So far the people feel satisfied in this respect, and we are not, of course, to mind any dissatisfaction expressed by those who wish to evade justice, but who are now compelled to submit to justice. This state of things must necessarily go on for some time, but there is ample scope for progressive improvement. We must gradually make laws of our own to some extent. In this respect, I will here indicate my views briefly and generally.

Adoption of the Indian Penal Code strongly recommended.

(12) I would strongly recommend our early adoption of the British Indian Penal Code. With a few modifications and omissions, I may assure Your Highness that it is a splendid code of the Penal Law. It is one of the most national codes of the sort in existence in the whole world. It is a better Penal Code than what is in use in England itself. It is a code which is the result of the experience and reflection of the most eminent Jurists of Asia, Europe and America. General crimes are universal, that is to say, they are taken as crimes not only in this or in that State, but in all civilized States,

The Indian Penal Code treats of such crimes or offences. It is therefore applicable to India and to any part of India. Indeed, it was framed for India itself. It has been applied to the wide regions of the British Indian Empire and has generally worked well. I am decidedly of opinion that we cannot do better than adopt it here, with, as I have already said, the requisite modifications and adaptations. These will be very few indeed.

(13) A similar course seems desirable in relation to Criminal Procedure with considerable simplification, and so on. In short, the broad lines I would recommend, are to go on with the administration of justice as at present, and to begin making laws gradually and from time to time, as it may be found necessary to do.

Also of the Criminal Procedure Code.

(14) Law and Justice generally and practically are subjects which Mr. Cursetji will deal with better than I can. I must not trench upon his field. But the few very general observations I am offering fall within the category of the fundamental principles of good government I am to communicate to Your Highness. I have said that we must begin to make regular laws gradually and from time to time as may be found necessary hereafter. In this important connection, I would suggest some points to be kept in view. They are as follows.

Regular laws must be made gradually.

21

(15). No existing custom which is fairly good and has long been recognised and acted upon by the people should be set aside or altered; strong sound reason must be shown for such action. The evil which is sought to be corrected must be clearly shown; what is the evil exactly; what is its magnitude; how many persons does it affect; do the people themselves complain of the evil; does the evil really diminish the happiness of the people which is the great object of good government? In short, unless the evil is so material that the people themselves or an intelligent portion of them would wish it to be remedied, leave the long established customary law as it is.

No good custom to be set aside.

(16) On the other hand, if the evil is clearly substantiated, so that there is no doubt about it, proceed to its remedy. Without this, there would be no progress—no improvement. What I have said about setting aside or altering existing customary law equally applies to setting aside or altering existing written law.

Remedy an evil custom.

(17) No new law should be passed in any haste. The utmost deliberation should precede the passing of any new law. See that the proposed law is not opposed to any fundamental principle recognized by civilized communities. If the proposed law be unique—be

No new law to be hastily passed.

utterly without analogy in civilized communities of modern times—suspect its soundness.

The proposed law to be discussed with the Ministers and Judges.

(18) Discuss the proposed law with the Principal Ministers, and the Principal Judges and some of the principal intelligent members of the general community and take their opinions. Consult also intelligent members of that part of the community which may be affected by the proposed law. Freely elicit objections in order that they may be known and may be duly weighed.

Agree with the majority.

(19) As a rule, do not pass any law which is opposed by the greater portion of those with whom you have fully discussed it. Indeed, it would be quite unsafe—it might be even dangerous for any Maharaja to pass any law or any part of a law, without at least some of his ministers and some of his judges assenting to the same, and being prepared to defend the same if assailed, and to be fully responsible for its soundness.

Adopt the analogy of the British Law. Copy the good of another.

(20) Adopt the analogy of the British Indian Law except where there are strong reasons to the contrary. Do not let any law differ from the corresponding British Indian Law merely for the unreasonable sake of showing independence or originality. This spirit would be petty and irrational. Never mind if certain people say that we

are merely copying. Provided the law itself is good and is applicable to our people, there can be nothing blameable in copying. One country may well adopt the good things of another. The most advanced—the proudest and the most independent nations—follow that course, otherwise the knowledge and experience of one country would become useless to another.

"Conflict of laws" not desirable.

(21) There is another strong reason to recommend that our laws should differ as little as possible from those of our neighbours, and it is this. If the important laws governing similar and adjacent communities, materially differ, there ensues what is called "conflict of laws" which brings great difficulties and perplexities in the administration of justice. The difficulties and perplexities are so numerous and so serious that they have been the subject of bulky volumes by some of the ablest jurists.

Law not to interfere with religion.

(22) Again, see that the proposed law does not trench upon the domain of religion. Every law should abstain from interference with the religious community concerned. The State should be neutral and impartial in its policy. The policy of the State should be to let every individual practise any religion he likes, provided he does not thereby injure others, that is to say, violate the rights of others.

(23) Again every proposed law must, more or less affect the liberty or property of the people—must curtail liberty or diminish property. This is an evil in itself. Make sure, before passing the law, that the good of it will be clearly in excess of the evil attended to, if not, the proposed law cannot be a good one.

It should do more good than evil.

(24) Make each law as simple and as intelligible to the people as may be possible consistently with the object to be accomplished. See that the proposed law does not unduly favour any particular section of the people at the expense of another section. The laws should be impartial to all sections.

It should be simple and impartial.

(25) See that the proposed law does not curtail, or curtails as little as possible, the liberty of any one to make himself as happy as he likes and in any manner he judges best—provided he does not injure others. As a rule, every member of society is the most interested in his own welfare. He will not neglect himself. His self-interest will powerfully prompt him to promote his own happiness. The State need not burden itself with any serious anxieties in this respect. The best policy for the State to pursue is to leave each individual to make himself happy in the manner he judges best—provided he does not injure another—

It should not curtail personal liberty.

provided, he leaves other individuals similar liberty. The more this principle is kept in view and acted upon, the greater will be the quantity of happiness earned by each individual, and hence the greater will be the total quantity of happiness earned by the whole community.

Avoid passing bad laws.

(26) I have thus given Your Highness a few hints—a few rough hints—which will generally enable you to avoid passing bad or objectionable laws. All those hints you may not be able to carry in your memory. But, as you are getting these notes copied in your book, you may refer to them when you have occasion to consider any proposed law.

The subject of regular law.

(27) I have still a few further observations to offer. Heretofore, many things have been done by the several departments by means of circular orders, Jahirnamas or Notifications. It was necessary to do so at this stage, the main object being to do away speedily with the darkness and confusion which had prevailed and to arrange things in a rough and ready manner, leaving nicer adjustments to follow at greater leisure. But hereafter, say from the time Your Highness will assume the powers of Maharaja, that every measure which affects or materially affects the person, property or liberty of the people should be the subject of regular law framed and passed in Your Highness'

name in due form. This will ensure greater precision and uniformity. It will carry greater weight. It will better enable the people to know what laws they are to obey and what the consequences of disobedience are. It will be a greater convenience to those officers themselves who have to give effect to the laws.

Do not give any order opposed to the laws.

(28) I beg Your Highness will always remember that the laws are the well-considered and permanent orders of the State. The Maharaja must not himself counteract them publicly or privately. The Maharaja must not give any orders opposed to the laws. He must not privately ask or hint to any judge or magistrate to favour or to disfavour any one by setting aside the law. I mention this particularly and emphatically because Maharajas are under great temptation to do what they must not do. It would be false and treacherous conduct for any Raja or Maharaja to pass a deliberate order in public in the shape of a law and to ask judges and magistrates privately to break that very order.

The more the laws are respected, the better.

(29) The more the laws are respected, the better it is for the happiness of the people, which is the first duty of the ruler. And the ruler himself must most respect the laws as an example to the people.

(30) Foolish, ignorant or selfish persons will constantly ask you—urge you—to do something yourself, or to get others to do something against the laws. They will even venture to say, "Is not the great Gaekwar able to do what he likes? "Is there any power to restrain the Maharaja himself?" "If there is, then the Maharaja is not supreme in his country. He is a timid or weak Maharaja," and so on. Such things will be told you constantly in one form or another. Your Highness must not allow yourself to be influenced or excited thereby in the least. Take it all coolly and calmly. With a gentle royal smile, answer them by saying, "My education and my reflection have convinced me that that Maharaja is truly great who constantly respects the laws which have been designed for the good of the people. I am determined to act under that conviction." By pursuing such a course you will become truly great. You will be the greatest benefactor of your people. You will have a high place in the history of your country.

Do not be influenced by foolish persons.

(48) It remains for me to say that the Hindu Shastras also repeatedly and most powerfully inculcate the same thing. One of their happiest maxims is that "Law is the king of kings." It is a precious maxim which must be engraved on the memory of rulers.

The Hindu Shastras on law.

CHAPTER XXIX

FUNDAMENTAL PRINCIPLES.—*Contd.*

Wednesday, 8th June, 1881.

A Maharaja is the depository of the greatest wealth and power and should devote himself to public good.

The great and fundamental truths which I have had the honour of offering for Your Highness' acceptance are the results of my sincere and thorough conviction. Those truths have been my guidance in the conduct of public affairs while filling the office of Chief Minister in three Native States successively for a series of more than twenty years. In following the guidance of those grand truths, in doing my best to assist in promoting the welfare of the people concerned, I have felt an inward satisfaction which words cannot adequately describe, but the like of which, I trust, Your Highness will yourself enjoy in all its plenitude. It is probably the purest and noblest of human pleasures. It is a pleasure that lasts to the end of life. It is a sublime maxim of the Vedas that he alone lives who lives to do good to others. Who can do more good to others than the Ruler of a community —than a Maharaja who is the depository of the greatest power and wealth in his country ? I have alluded to myself personally, not in a spirit of self-praise, but with the view of strengthening your impressions. If an humble private individual like myself has been liberally rewarded with honour and distinction in consequence of faithful endeavours to promote the happiness of the people, you may easily conceive what brilliant and lasting fame will be your reward as a Maharaja devoting himself to public good. But there is a far brighter reward to be looked for than worldly praise and fame. I refer to that great source which ordained your exaltation to your present position and opportunities.

The ideas of Vathel.

(2) In advising Your Highness in the interests of good government, let me call to my aid an eminent teacher of mankind in general and of Princes in particular. I refer to Vathel, a famous European author, who lived in the last century. The following are some of his ideas bearing on the topics I have already submitted to Your Highness :—

A good Prince will not seek his own satisfaction.

" A good Prince, a wise conductor of society, ought to have his mind impressed with this great truth that the Sovereign power is solely entrusted to him for the safety of the State and the happiness of all the people ; that he is not permitted to consider himself as the principal object in the administration of affairs, to seek his own satisfaction, or his private advantage, but that he ought to direct all his views, all his steps, to the greatest advantage of the State and people who have submitted to him.

* * * * *

Criminal flattery and posts given by favour, to the neglect of merit.

"But in most kingdoms a criminal flattery has long since caused these maxims to be forgotten. A crowd of servile courtiers easily persuade a proud monarch that the nation was made for him and not he for the nation. He soon considers the kingdom as a patrimony that is his own property and his people as a herd of cattle from which he is to derive his wealth and which he may dispose of to answer his own views and gratify his passions. Hence those fatal wars undertaken by ambition, restlessness, hatred and pride. Hence those oppressive taxes, whose produce is dissipated by ruinous luxury, or squandered upon mistresses and favourites; hence, in fine, are important posts given by favour, while public merit is neglected and everything that does not immediately interest the Prince is abandoned to Ministers and subalterns. Who can, in this unhappy government, discover an authority established for the public welfare? A great Prince will be on his guard even against his virtues. Let us not say, with some writers, that private virtues are not the virtues of kings—a maxim of superficial politicians, or of those who are very inaccurate in their expressions goodness, friendship, gratitude, are still virtues on the throne ; and would to God they were always to be found there ! But a wise king does not yield an undeserving obedience to their impulse. He cherishes them, he cultivates them in his private life, but in State affairs he listens only to justice and sound policy. And why ? Because he knows that the government was entrusted to him only for the happiness of society, and that, therefore, he ought not to consult his own pleasure in the use he makes of his power. He tempers his goodness with wisdom, he gives to friendship his domestic and private favours ; he distributes posts and employments according to merit, public rewards to services done to the State. In a word, he uses the public power only with a view to the public welfare.

* * *

He is the guardian of the laws.

"He is, by virtue of that power, the guardian and defender of the laws ; and while it is his duty to restrain each daring violater of them, ought he himself to trample them under foot ?

* * *

He should submit to the laws himself.

"But while these laws exist, the sovereign ought religiously to maintain and observe them. They are the foundation of the public tranquillity and the firmest support of the sovereign authority.

Everything is uncertain, violent, and subject to revolutions in those unhappy States where arbitrary power has placed her throne. It is, therefore, the true interest of the Prince, as well as his duty, to maintain and respect the laws; he ought to submit to them himself. We find this truth established in a piece published by order of Louis XIV, one of the most absolute Princes that ever reigned in Europe. "Let it not be said that the sovereign is not subject to the laws of his States, since the contrary proposition is one of the truths of the law of nations which flattery has sometimes attacked and which good princes have always defended as a tutelar divinity of their States."

* * *

(3) I will now proceed to quote a passage or two of similar effect from Manu, the great Hindu Law-giver :—

Manu, on the duties of the king.

He says, "Let the king act a father to his people."

Again, "Let the king prepare a just compensation for the good, and a just punishment for the bad. The rule of strict justice let him never transgress."

Again, "A king is pronounced equally unjust in releasing the man who deserves punishment, and in punishing the man who deserves it not. He is just who always inflicts the punishment ordained by law."

(4) All this eminently shows that kings have high duties and responsibilities ;—that they are not to act wildly and arbitrarily like wild animals ;—that they have great principles and rules to respect. Their great duty is to promote the happiness of the people over whom the Almighty has placed them.

Kings have high duties and responsibilities.

(5) To promote the happiness of the people is an object easily enough understood in the gross, but it requires much study and it costs much self-denial to effectuate that object in these times when the interests of the people have become very numerous and very complex and when good government has become a regular science and also an art which needs to be regularly learnt. Principles and rules of good government have to be carefully learnt. They have to be constantly respected and observed. In other words, it is not enough for a Maharaja to say, "I know that it is my duty to be a father to my people" and to proceed to act under the capricious impulses of an untutored common sense. The fact is, the Maharaja has to learn his high profession and to practice it in conformity with its great laws and rules. The Maharaja who does not accept and observe such laws and rules will be just like a navigator in charge of a big ship, who refuses the guidance of the compass and of the chart.

Good government is a science and an art.

Why Oudh was annexed.

(6) I have already submitted to you some important quotations from authority in order to strengthen the impressions I desire to make on your mind. I will here invite Your Highness's attention to a few more quotations and these are taken from papers relating to the recent annexation of the large and important country of Oudh. I have laid great stress on the rulers' duty of maintaining the security of life, person, liberty and property and have pointed out the means to be employed to effect that object. The Rulers of Oudh greatly failed in that object, and this was one of the strongest grounds for the annexation of that territory, as seen from the following extracts from the Oudh papers.

(a) The officers incompetent and the ruler's disregard to his duties.

(a) The Resident of Oudh reports: "In spite of all that I have urged upon His Majesty (the King of Oudh) he continues to confide the conduct of his affairs to the same worthless and incompetent characters; to devote all his time to personal gratifications and frivolous amusements; and to manifest the same utter disregard to his duties and high responsibilities. The same insecurity of life and property in all parts of his dominions is felt, the same maladministration and malversations prevail in all departments."

(*b*) In another part, the Resident says: "It was not to be wondered at that the young Nawab on his accession to power, with low people about him, and with only that degree of education which Native Princes receive, considered himself as having arrived at the highest of earthly felicity, and wondering what bonds and laws were to curb the will of a king, etc."

(*b*) The Nawab with low associates and no education.

(*c*) Again, the Resident reported to the Governor-General, "of judicial courts there are none except at the Capital and those which are there maintained are of no value."

(c) Absence of judicial courts.

(*d*) The consequence of this was that the administration of justice in Oudh was miserable. It is instructive to observe how the Government of India took notice of a case in which a person was, through influence, allowed to go unpunished, though there was clear evidence to prove that he had committed murder. The Government of India wrote, on the occasion, to the Resident at Lucknow in the following words :—

The administration miserable.

"You will demand an audience of the King. You will represent to His Majesty the indignation with which the Governor-General views the scandalous denial of justice, which has just been exhibited at Lucknow, in the acquittal of this murderer, in the face of the clearest proofs of his guilt. And you will add that such acts are rapidly filling up the measures of the King's misgovernment, which, His Majesty has been already warned, must end in the entire subversion of his kingly power."

(e) Even the British subjects suffered.

(*e*) The Resident also complained that in consequence of want of administration of justice in Oudh, the subjects of the British Government, who were in that territory, also suffered. The British Government could not remain indifferent when their own subjects thus suffered from the maladministration of justice in Oudh.

(*f*) No efficient Police.

(*f*) The Resident also complained that there was no efficient Police in Oudh territories. To quote again from the Oudh papers: "Under the present regime, I do not think there is a shadow of security for life or property in Oudh. In this part of the country, it is almost impossible for people to travel, unless escorted by a large body of armed men."

A Raj without any security of life, person and property must fall.

(7) I hope that I have now said enough and quoted enough, to produce an unshakeable conviction, in Your Highness' mind, of the vital importance of an efficient Police supported by a Military force, and of the vital importance of an efficient adminis-

tration of justice. Without these there can be no security of life, person, liberty, or property. And I say emphatically that, without such security, a Raj must inevitably fall, the fall being only a question of time. Fall, it must, sooner or later.

Let these convictions be handed down to posterity.

(8) As one of the warmest well-wishers of Native States—as one, who most earnestly desires that the existing Native States should ever continue to live—I will not be satisfied with Your Highness' entertaining and cherishing the convictions above-mentioned; but I entreat Your Highness to take the utmost pains to communicate your conviction to your children with injunctions to them to communicate those convictions to their children again, so that, there may never arise any break in the continuity of those convictions in the Gaekwar House. Let every ruler of Baroda—good or bad or indifferent—maintain fair security of life, person, liberty and property in these territories and I guarantee the perpetuity of the Baroda Raj.

If such security is not maintained, rulers will lose their sovereign power.

(9) On the other hand, if the Native States fail to maintain such security, I predict that their rulers will, sooner or later, one after another lose sovereign power and subside into the states of mere wealthy Jamindars. It is a contingency,

most painful to contemplate, but it must be foreseen in order that it may be averted. (The proverb says: "To be forewarned is to be forearmed.")

A most important piece of public service.

(10) It is on these grounds that the administration during Your Highness' minority has taken decided and vigorous action by way of organizing an efficient police and an efficient system of administering justice—calculated to establish fair security of life, person, liberty and property. We consider this a most important and most essential piece of public service performed. We are proud of the action taken.

Those who ruin Native States.

(11) If, therefore, any one, under the influence of ignorance or of a factious spirit, tells Your Highness that we have done wrong in this respect—that we have done wrong in incurring the cost of establishing the police and the judicial machinery—and advise you to do away with these and to revert to the old state of things, Your Highness should regard him as unfit to take part in your counsels. Such persons are just those who have already unconsciously ruined some Native States, and they are just those who will yet similarly ruin others.

The mistakes of former times.

(12) In connexion with the subject in hand, I must draw Your Highness' attention to one of the grave conclusions

which Sir R. Meade's Commission has recorded against Malhar Rao Gaekwar, the then ruler of Baroda, namely, "That the judicial department and administration require entire reform, the existing abuses being abolished so as to remove the present uncertain and irregular application of the law and want of confidence in the proceedings of the courts and magistrates."

How the judicial Department is established on a firm basis.

(13) The entire reform pointed out by the commission has been happily effected in its main features—one proof of this is to be found in the following passage extracted from a recent report of the Agent to the Governor-General to the Government of India, namely—"The Judicial Department of the State is now established on a firm basis. It is sufficient for the work, is well paid, is officered, except in some of the posts in the lower grades by thoroughly qualified men, and the work is done generally in a highly satisfactory manner. The Judges of the Varisht Court and of the Session Courts would do credit to any service. There is, of course, still room for improvement in regard to despatch and precision. There is certainly no branch of the administration which gives greater satisfaction to the people than the Judicial."

(14). It will thus be seen, beyond all doubt, that it will be Your Highness' most important duty to maintain the progress so far made, and to make further possible improvements. I beg Your Highness to thoroughly digest and assimilate the general and special points I have been endeavouring to impress upon you.

Its progress to be maintained.

CHAPTER XXX.

FUNDAMENTAL PRINCIPLES.—(*contd.*)

PUBLIC HEALTH.

Wednesday, 22nd June, 1881.

The first object of good Government.

I have dwelt somewhat longer on the subject of the security of life, person, liberty and property, because it is the condition of pre-eminent importance to the well-being of the people—the well-being of the people being the first object of good government. Unless a government has established and will steadily maintain such security, it cannot claim to be good—the ruler cannot say he has done his duty to the people.

The next duty is to maintain the people in good health—public health.

(2) The next important duty of government is to do what may be possible to maintain the people in good health. The health of each individual in a community depends in a great measure, on himself—on his food, clothing, exercise, medical treatment etc. As every one has naturally a very strong desire to enjoy the blessing of health, he may be expected himself to take care of his health. But there are some important matters connected with public health which individuals cannot insure. They are matters which the governments alone

can properly arrange. If the government do not take up such matters they will not be attended to at all. I will now proceed to state the chief of such matters.

Sanitation.

(3) Where people live in numbers and close to each other as in cities and towns, cleanliness has to be maintained as an important condition of public health. Dirt and refuse have to be removed from the streets. The drains have to be kept in good order. Abundance of fresh air has to be let in—and so forth. All this is called sanitation. With this may be combined several arrangements for public convenience comfort, and safety. For example, good carriage roads may be made. The roads may be watered and lighted. Appliances may be kept ready to put down fires.

A sufficient and pure water-supply.

(4) Another measure of great importance to public health is to give the people a sufficient and pure supply of water for daily use. In tropical climates, this is one of the most valued of blessings. The Maharaja who confers this blessing is sure to live in the memory of a grateful people.

Airy places for recreation.

(5) Another measure conducive to public health is to give to the crowded inhabitants of the city some pleasant and airy places to which they can drive, ride or walk ; and where they can spend some portion of their leisure

during the morning or evening with great benefit to their health. The Race-course and the Public Park in this city of Baroda are examples of such places of resort.

Vaccination.

(6) Another measure conducive to public health is to arrange for the vaccination of the people and the consequent prevention of the dreadful attacks of small-pox.

Hospitals.

(7) Another measure conducive to public health is to establish, at the various centres of population, Hospitals and Dispensaries, where sick persons may easily obtain medical advice, medical treatment, and the requisite medicines themselves.

The health of the people, a subject of primary importance.

(8) Any Government which cares for the happiness of the people will earnestly attend to all these measures and, perhaps, to others also of the kind which I need not stop here to specify. Money spent on such measures is always well spent. The people have an undoubted right to be thus protected in their health. The Maharaja, who acts as the father of his people, will always cheerfully arrange for the health of his people.

Action already taken.

(9) During Your Highness' minority therefore, the administration has taken some action in this important direction. The city of Baroda, your capital, is now cleaner than before. It has better roads, it is

better watered and better lighted. It is more efficiently protected against fires. The people have the Race-course and the new Public Park to take fresh air in. Vaccination is better attended to, and good Medical Institutions have been established and are well maintained. Towns in the Talooks have also had some attention paid to them in these respects. For more detailed information as to what has been heretofore done, I beg to refer Your Highness to the Administration Reports.

There is scope for further action.

(10) But it is certain that we are yet far from the complete fulfilment of our duty in this branch. There is much scope for further action, to which, I trust, Your Highness will turn your attention among other important things. Much yet remains to be done, and all this will be brought to your notice in detail hereafter. But I will here mention one or two salient points.

A water-supply scheme for Baroda.

(11) It is most unfortunate that we have not been able to provide a good water-supply for this city of Baroda though most anxious to do so. Large and costly undertakings require to be very carefully investigated before proceeding to execution. This is the only way of avoiding blunders and losses. A thorough investigation was therefore instituted in order to ascertain what alternative projects

were available. It was made by employing exclusively for the purpose Mr. Crossthwaite, a Bengal Engineer specially versed in the water-supply of towns and cities. The result may be briefly stated. Water cannot be brought to this city from the Nerbuda river, nor from the Oorsang tributary of the Nerbuda, nor from the Mahi river, nor from Pawagar, nor from the Muwar Talao near Saoli. The only project open was declared to be that of sinking two or three gigantic wells near the Railway station, drawing water from them by means of powerful steam machinery, storing up the water to a certain extent, and distributing the same through the city in the usual manner. Here the matter has rested for some time. This project involves certain risk and uncertainty which will be explained to Your Highness when the subject is seriously taken up for consideration. I will, therefore, only say that if Your Highness succeeds in giving the city a good water-supply, Your Highness will, on this account alone, be remembered as a great benefactor.

The drainage.

(12) The improvement of the drainage of the city is another very important question. It is really one of the most difficult and puzzling questions.

Improvements in other towns.

(13) In other towns, those in the Talooks—we have as yet confined ourselves to the maintenance of cleanliness

and even this has been,I am afraid, very superficial. In the town of Nowsari, however, much has been done in comparison. Some lakhs of rupees have been sanctioned for securing good drinking water wells for the various villages throughout these territories, and the work is, I believe, already commenced. It has to be urged on to completion. Hospitals and Dispensaries and Vaccinating Agencies have been fairly spread over the country. In connection with this subject, I beg to say that whatever is done to promote the health of the people to prevent disease and to cure or mitigate suffering cannot fail to be appreciated as one of the most direct and practical benefits of good government. A benevolent Ruler will give a large share of his attention to the promotion of public health, which is a very important component element of public happiness, the main object of government.

(14) In our anxiety to promote public health, we have, however, to be careful not to interfere unnecessarily with the liberty of the individual —a liberty which is one of the most valuable blessings. The individual must not be forced to take particular diet, to take particular medicines,to take particular exercise, etc. Of these the individual himself is the best judge. The government will do well to limit its action to matters which affect the community in

Individual liberty not to be interfered with, to promote public health.

the gross—such as general cleanliness, good drainage, good water-supply, good hospitals and dispensaries, efficient vaccine operations, etc., etc. In these matters the government acts as representing the community itself, and for the benefit of the community.

The public good and popular resistance are both points to be considered.

(15) Even while thus acting, the Government has to be careful that it is not carried too far by its benevolent zeal—that it does not go too much in advance of the views and wishes of the people in the present state of their intelligence and education. How far the government may go and when it should stop, in a given case, are practical questions which will have to be decided from time to time after a careful comparison of the public good proposed to be affected on the one hand, with the popular resistance which might be expected on the other hand.

Government may give useful advice.

(16) I have said above that in the matter of health the liberty of the individual should not be unnecessarily interfered with. But, without interfering with that liberty, Government may give usual advice. For instance, Government in the Medical department may notify to the people that such and such precautions are instrumental in averting attacks of cholera—that, when an attack actually occurs, such and such a remedy has been found to be good

—that such and such precautions are useful to prevent the spread of the disease—and so forth.

Special preventive and curative measures.

(17) Whenever any general diseases break out, such as cholera, fever, small-pox, etc., the Government should take special preventive and curative measures. For instance, additional medical men should be sent off for acting in the locality concerned. Medicines should be made available to the people concerned. The Medical Department will propose the necessary measures, and these must be promptly sanctioned.

The Medical Department, the best adviser.

(18) In matters relating to public health generally, the Medical Department is the best adviser of the government.

Maintain the Medical institutions.

(19) After all that I have said about public health, I am sure your Highness will readily recognize the great duty of maintaining and in no way curtailing the various Medical Institutions which have been brought into existence during your minority and which are largely saving life, promoting health and mitigating suffering. The father of the people must never say, "Never mind how the people get sick, suffer, and die—I want to save some money by abolishing or reducing these Medical Institutions." I do hope that the great Gaekwar house will never produce so avaricious and cruel a father of the people.

A summary to show the great duties of the Government.

(20) I will close this day's lecture here by a very brief retrospect.

(*i*) We began by saying that the first duty of the government is to promote the happiness of the people.

(*ii*) We recognized the fact that the security of life, person, liberty and property is indispensably necessary to the happiness of the people.

(*iii*) We saw how necessary it is for this important object to maintain a sufficient and efficient Police, to maintain a moderate and effective military force, to maintain a well-organized and efficient judicial machinery and to uphold and enforce the laws with firmness and impartiality.

(*iv*) And to-day, we have seen how important it is for public happiness to maintain and improve sanitation in towns and cities and to maintain and improve the various medical agencies which are at work—in a word, to maintain and improve the health of the population.

We do well, occasionally, to thus briefly review the leading principles we have already dwelt upon, because it strengthens the impressions made, it shows in a small compass what the great duties of the government are, it shows them in the order of their importance, and it shows their mutual relations.

CHAPTER XXXI.

FUNDAMENTAL PRINCIPLES.—(*contd*).

Wednesday 30th June, 1881.

Another important duty—the supply of food.

The last time we met here, we dwelt on the duty of the government to promote the health of the people and briefly noticed the principal methods in which this may be done. We will now proceed to another very important duty of government, namely, the duty of doing all that may be possible to enable the people to obtain sufficient and even abundant food. Without sufficient food, the people, it is obvious, cannot be happy.

Individual exertion.

(2) I may observe at the outset that, in this respect, the government cannot do much. Much must be left to the exertions of the people themselves. Each member of the community has to work for himself and family and to thereby earn the means of living. Nature has made food so absolutely necessary to every one, that every one may be expected to do his utmost to acquire food without being urged to do so from the outside. In short, natural motives act with great force in this direction.

(3) Natural motives prompt individuals to acquire not only food, but many other things which are the means of happiness. The main duty of the government is to let those motives act with all legitimate freedom, to see that those natural motives are not needlessly impeded or weakened by artificial causes. This duty of government should be clearly realized and steadily fulfilled.

Government to see that the natural motives act freely.

(4) Let us here consider what the government should do and what it should not do, in order to let those natural motives operate fully and bear all good fruit. As I have already stated, every member of a community is prompted by natural motives to acquire the means of his own happiness. Prompted by such motives he will employ his best exertions to acquire wealth. Now government should, by maintaining security of life, person, liberty and property, maintain those natural motives in all their strength, allow free scope for those exertions, and secure that wealth fully to the acquirer. Just see what would take place if there were little or no security of life, person, liberty and property. Many a man would say to himself, " why should I acquire wealth, or to acquire it why should I save anything while I am liable to be murdered at any time, or wounded or thrown into prison, or despoiled of my wealth." It follows, then, the security of life,

The security of life, etc., necessary for the acquisition of wealth.

person, liberty and property is necessary for the acquisition and growth of wealth in the community. The people should have no fears of the sort indicated above. I will state the matter somewhat more in detail. No one should have reason to fear that he might be plundered of his property whether in town, or in country, or on the high-way. The sowkar must be secured in the possession of his money. The ryot must be secured in the possession of his stock of grain; even the poor woman who carries a basket of vegetables to the market must feel secure as regards those vegetables. In short, every one, rich and poor, must feel that he is pretty sure of keeping and enjoying his property, great or small. He must feel secure against violence, against fraud, against unjust litigation and arbitrary action by the Sarkar.

How these conditions will be secured.

(5) All these conditions will be secured by the means I have already explained, namely, by maintaining a good Police in villages and towns, by maintaining an efficient judicial machinery and by maintaining good laws. The government should do many other things in order to promote the growth of wealth, and I will proceed to state some of them.

Let the people enjoy their wealth freely.

(6) The government should allow the people to enjoy their wealth freely, that is to say without needless restrictions or fears. For example, I say, no one should be

prevented from driving a carriage and pair. Again, no one should be prevented from building the firmest houses by the sides of the high roads. Again, no one should be prevented from wearing rich clothes or costly ornaments. In short, the people should be quite free to enjoy or display their wealth as they may like. Indeed, the happier the Maharaja sees his people, the happier should he himself be.

Importance of the administration with respect to the ryots and to land.

(7) To proceed to another matter of importance. A large portion of our people derive their subsistence from the cultivation of soil. The land is a great source of wealth. The ryot labours on the land and the land gives him a return. It follows that the Administration with respect to the ryot and with respect to the land has a very important bearing on the happiness of our subjects. It should be remembered that the ryots—those who pursue agriculture as their profession —form the great body of our subjects who reside permanently in the country, who are the fixed population. As the land they cultivate is immoveable, they, the cultivators, are also in a great measure immoveable. As a body, the ryots would not think of abandoning their lands and of leaving the country unless great and continued *zooloom* was practised. The ryots, then, constitute a very important portion of our settled population, and the produce they raise every year from the land constitutes a very important

portion of the wealth of the country. Hence the great importance of the Administration with respect to the ryots and with respect to the land.

Taxes to be moderate.

(8) To make the ryots happy and to promote the growth of wealth from land, the Sarkar's tax on the land should be moderate, so moderate as to leave to the ryots enough to maintain themselves and their families in fair comfort. In many Native States, the principle practically followed is unfortunately more or less different. Some of these States wring as large a revenue as possible from the ryots—and this, of course, impoverishes this very useful class of subjects. It is quite contrary to the fundamental maxim with which we started, namely, it is the first object of government to promote the happiness of the people.

The ryots should have a good tenure.

(9) Another important thing necessary to make the ryots happy and to promote the growth of wealth from land, is that the ryots should have a good tenure for holding the land. The ryots should feel every confidence that they will not be deprived of their land so long as they regularly pay the Sarkar tax due thereon. The ryots should feel that, provided they pay the tax regularly, they can hold the land for generations. It has been proved by reasoning, and it has been found by experience, that nothing is more prejudicial to agricultural prosperity than nsecurity of possession.

(10) Another important thing necessary to make the ryots happy and to promote the growth of wealth from land, is that, when the land is made to yield more in consequence of the application to the land of the ryots' labour and capital, the Sarkar should not increase its tax on that account and thereby deprive the ryots of the fair return due to their labour and capital. If the Sarkar pursues a contrary policy, the ryots will feel no inducement to lay out their labour and capital for the improvement of the land; the yield of the land will not increase and may even decrease.

Taxation not to be increased.

(11) Another important thing necessary to make the ryots happy and to promote the growth of wealth from land is that Izardars or farmers of revenue should not be employed between the ryots and the Sarkar. Such agents used to be extensively employed in former times, and they used to oppress and impoverish the ryots terribly. The best system is that known as the Ryotwari, that is to say, that system under which the Sarkar deals with each ryot directly. This system is really most favourable to the ryot; it secures him the best justice and the best consideration, and promotes his self-respect and independence. The only thing is that such a system will require the employment of an extensive agency and an agency most carefully

Do not employ farmers of revenue between the ryots and the Sarkar.

selected with reference to knowledge, experience, judgment and probity. The cost of such agency will be more than re-paid by the saving of what the Izardar would otherwise have pocketed, while an immense advantage is that the ryots will be protected against heavy and arbitrary exactions.

Bhag-Batai system not desirable.

(12) I must take this opportunity to impress another truth on Your Highness' mind. Kazi Sahib has, no doubt, explained to you what the Bhag-Batai system is. Its main feature is that the Sarkar takes actually a portion of the produce of the land as the Sarkar's revenue, instead of taking the revenue in cash. The result of my consideration of this system is that, though it may answer for States, it would not at all answer for a large State like Baroda. It has happily been mostly got rid of in these territories. The credit of this belongs to the late Maharaja Khande Rao. I hope that the great and beneficial change which that Maharaja introduced will be fully maintained. In the Amreli Mahals, however, the Bhag-Batai system still continues. Some steps have been taken to apply a corrective in this respect.

A regular survey and re-assessment necessary.

(13) I have already brought to Your Highness' notice the great importance of the land tax being moderate. To fix the land-tax moderately and equitably,

a regular survey and re-assessment are indispensably necessary. It is an operation of great magnitude and great cost, but, I repeat, it is quite necessary. The present Administration has had no leisure to undertake that operation. But I hope that so necessary a measure will not be long delayed, for on it the welfare of the great body of the ryots largely depends.

Arbitrary taxes not to be imposed.

(14) When the land tax has been moderately and equitably fixed by means of the operation just alluded to, the Maharaja should most resolutely abstain from super-adding arbitrary and unjust taxes like the gadi nazrana, palace nazrana, marriage nazrana, and so forth.

Grant of special privileges objectionable.

(15) I would also warn Your Highness against another abuse. It has happened that some individual of religious or other influences came to the Maharaja and applied for an annual subsidy. Instead of disposing of the matter in some ordinary way, it has sometimes happened the Maharaja issued a sanad authorizing the said individual to levy a tax on each ryot or on each plough of a ryot in a certain village or in a certain group of villages. The grant of such a right or privilege is most objectionable, because injurious to the ryots concerned. I hope that such grants will never be made hereafter. By giving effect to the leading principles

I have mentioned, the ryots will be made happy and the land will yield wealth steadily and to the greatest possible extent. I have, however, to draw Your Highness' attention to one or two more matters in the same connection.

Agricultural produce not to be taxed, when exported.

(16) I think it is essential to agricultural prosperity that agricultural produce should not be burdened with any heavy duties when the same is exported. If the produce could be altogether freed from export duty, this would be the best thing. But if circumstances make this difficult, the export duty must be very moderate. I should say, generally, that the duty should be as much as possible below 5 per cent. on the value of the commodity exported. Special articles such as opium, etc., are, of course, exceptions to the general principle.

Food-grains to be free from duty.

(17) It being desirable that food should be cheap to all, and especially to the poorer classes, I think that all food-grains should be free from duty altogether.

Encourage the multiplication of production.

(18) Again. Any measures which tend to increase the produce of the land, or to make the produce more valuable are most beneficial. Produce is increased, for instance, by better ploughing, better manuring, better weeding, etc. More valuable crops may be raised by providing or improving the

means of irrigation. By such means, land which has been yielding some poor crop may, for example, be made to yield sugarcane. Instead of yielding 20 Rupees' worth of crop per acre, it may be made to yield 200 Rupees' worth—an immense gain to the ryot individually and to the people generally. Hence the Sarkar should do everything possible to encourage the multiplication of wells and other means of irrigation.

Reduce the cost of carriage.

(19) Again. The great bulk of agricultural produce has to be carried to the market for sale. The charge for such carriage may seem small in individual cases, but, on the whole, it is a serious item. It follows that any measure which will reduce the cost of carriage will be a great benefit to the ryot and to the community. Therefore, the Sarkar should make roads of different classes, according to local requirements and resources, and should even make rail-roads where ever suitable. It should be remembered that when produce has to be carried on the heads of coolies, the cost of carriage is highest; when pack bullocks carry the produce, the cost of carriage is lowered; when carts carry the produce, especially on metalled roads, the cost of carriage is still further lowered. And carriage of produce by railway is the cheapest of the whole.

Give the ryots waste land on easy terms.

(20) Another means of increasing the production of land in a country is to have rules by which the ryots of the country are enabled to obtain waste land on easy terms and on a secure tenure.

Encourage Manufactures.

(21) But, besides land, there are other sources of wealth. Manufactures form the most important of these; manufactures supply the means of living to a portion of the population. As such, manufactures must be encouraged in every legitimate manner. This is all the more imperative because the population is increasing and there is not land enough to occupy all the population. That part of the population which cannot get land to cultivate must have recourse to manufactures. It follows that the Sarkar should not tax the manufactures of the country. If the Sarkar must tax to some extent, the tax must be very moderate indeed—it must be so moderate as not to repress or restrict the manufactures to an appreciable degree.

Do not tax raw materials or the machinery used.

(22) Again. To promote the manufactures of the country, the Sarkar should refrain from taxing the raw materials used in such manufactures, for taxing the raw materials would be indirectly, but in effect taxing the manufactures themselves. Similarly to promote the same object, all machinery used for local manufactures should be free from Sarkari

taxes. So also coal which may be necessary to make the machinery go. I say this particularly in reference to any spinning and weaving mills which may be introduced in these territories.

Government not to come in the way of the people undertaking any profitable work.

(23) Bearing on the general subject of the Sarkar affording every facility to the people in view to their finding employment—to their getting the means of livelihood—to their acquiring wealth—I may here allude to another principle. It is that the Sarkar should generally abstain from undertaking any work which would otherwise be done by the people themselves. To the extent the Sarkar undertakes such work, the people are deprived of the same and deprived of the profits thereby arising. It is, in fact, taking so much livelihood from the people. To elucidate this, I will give only one example. Suppose the Sarkar undertakes a system of lending money at interest to the people—in other words, that the Sarkar undertakes the business of the sowcar. It is evident that by so doing, the Sarkar deprives a certain number of sowcars of the means of their livelihood.

Do not undertake private trade.

(24) For the same reasons it would be wrong for the Sarkar to undertake private trade. Some Native princes have been so grasping, or so ignorant, that they have, contrary to the general principle

under advertency, undertaken a great deal of employment which ought to be left to the people themselves. Such princes, no doubt, obtain more money thereby, but it is at the expense of their people.

(25) To sum up—

Summary of the above.

To promote the acquisition of livelihood by the people—to promote the production of wealth in the country—the following are the chief conditions to be observed :—

(*a*) Security of life, person, liberty and property should be maintained.

(*b*) The people should be allowed to enjoy wealth freely.

(*c*) Land being the chief source of wealth, the Sarkari tax on land should be moderate.

(*d*) The tenure of land should be secured.

(*e*) The improvements made in land at the cost of the labour and capital of the ryots should not be taxed by the Sarkar—at least for a long time.

(*f*) The Ryotwari system of land administration is the best; the farming system—that of employing Izardars as formerly—is very pernicious.

(*g*) The Bhag-Batai system is bad for a large Native State like Baroda.

(*h*) A regular survey and re-assessment of lands should be made.

(*i*) There should be no arbitrary taxes like the gadi nazarana, etc.

(*j*) There should be no grants to priests, etc., of the privilege of levying imposts on ploughs, etc.

(*k*) Produce should not be charged with export duties. At least such duties should be very moderate.

(*l*) All food-grains required for the sustenance of our people should be free from duties altogether.

(*m*) All facilities should be afforded for the better ploughing, better manuring, better weeding, etc., of the land.

(*n*) Wells and other means of irrigation should be encouraged.

(*o*) Roads and railways should be made to reduce the cost of carriage.

(*p*) The ryots of the country should be enabled to get waste land for cultivation on easy terms and on good tenure.

(*q*) Manufactures should be encouraged.

(*r*) The manufactures of the country should not be taxed. If taxed, the tax should be very moderate indeed.

(*s*) The raw materials required for those manufactures should not be taxed.

(*t*) Machinery, coal, etc., required for the manufactures should not be taxed.

(u) The Sarkar should not undertake the work or trade which belongs to private individuals. In a few exceptional cases, however, where individuals would not come forward unless the Sarkar takes the initiative, the Sarkar might for a time do this.

The work of the present administration.

(26) The foregoing is not an exhaustive list, but it will indicate the general policy to be pursued and the reasons for pursuing the same. The matter being studied so far, other measures may suggest themselves hereafter. The broad principles being understood, it will be easy to discuss the merits of any new measure that may be brought forward for consideration. The present Administration has kept these general principles in view and endeavoured to give effect to several of them, more or less. But much yet remains to be accomplished in the same direction.

CHAPTER XXXII.

PUBLIC WORKS DEPARTMENT.

Wednesday, 13*th July*, 1881.

Observations on the Public Works Department.

To-day I will submit to Your Highness some observations on the Public Works Department, which has an important bearing on the public welfare.

A professional engineer to be at the head.

(2) This department constructs and repairs all important public works, such as Palaces, Jails, Schools, Hospitals, Dispensaries, Military buildings, roads and so forth. As such, it is necessary that a professional engineer should be at the head of this department.

Important Department that gives us useful public works.

(3) It is an important spending department. It spends several lakhs of rupees every year and gives us in return useful public works such as those above enumerated. What it spends in any year depends on the requirements of the State and also on what funds the State can spare from the surplus revenue—that is to say, the savings of the State. No State like Baroda can get on without the Public Works Department, because there are always valuable public works to be maintained in repair

without which those works would go to ruin more or less rapidly; and because there are also some new bridges to be constructed and so on.

Want of public works at the commencement of the administration.

(4) When the present administration began, we found that many public works of the most necessary character were wanting. There was not even a Cutcherry for the Dewan and for the heads of the various departments of the States. There were no Court-houses. There were nothing like proper Jails, School-houses, Hospitals, or Dispensaries; they were either very deficient or totally wanting. There was almost an entire absence of roads. The requirements of civilized government in these respects had been neglected by the State, for how many years I do not know. We experienced grave and numerous difficulties We therefore organised the Public Works Department and set it going. Many public works have been already finished, many are in progress, and some are in contemplation. The particulars may be learnt from the Administration Reports.

A few general principles.

(5) I proceed to lay before Your Highness some general principles which deserve to be kept in view in connection with this important department.

(*a*) A trained head.

(*a*) This important department always requires a professionally trained and qualified head as, indeed, every important department requires. Men like Gulam Ali of the old *Imarat Karkhana* would never do hereafter.

(b) A good Account and Audit Department.

(*b*) There should be a good account and audit establishment in connection with the Public Works Department to duly register and check every rupee of the expenditure. This Department should be readily supplied with the requisite funds. Failure in this respect would keep the Department more or less idle, which would be bad economy.

(c) Employ the best architect, for a costly building.

(*c*) Where a large, costly, and conspicuous building has to be erected, especially at the Capital, employ the best architect available to make proper designs and plans for the same. This is of the highest importance. Without such precaution, lakhs of rupees would be wasted—perhaps worse than wasted—because crude and clumsy edifices would be raised as monuments of the sad want of judgment of those who raised them.

(d) Do not blindly adopt European styles.

(*d*) Do not blindly adopt European styles for such buildings. European styles are best for Europe. We, in India, should follow the best styles which are suited to India, and which have been for ages adopted in India. In this respect, the course we have already taken in the instances of the new Palace, the new College and the new Jamnabai

Dispensary is the only proper one, and ought to serve as an example for the future.

(*e*) Plans and estimates to be previously prepared.

(*e*) As a rule, no public work should be begun without a plan and estimate previously prepared and submitted and sanctioned by the Sarkar. Whatever public work is undertaken, let it be done in the best manner. The work should be sound and durable and should reflect credit on the period in eyes of future generations. No trouble and expense should be spared to secure this great object.

(*f*) Get work done by contract.

(*f*) Get works executed by contract as far as may be possible. The contract system has many advantages over the departmental system.

(*g*) Prefer our labourers to outsiders.

(*g*) As far as may be possible, make our public works conducive to the livelihood of our labourers and artisans. Employ them in preference to outsiders. Employ local material in preference to foreign material.

(*h*) Do necessary repairs.

(*h*) Do not grudge the cost of necessary repairs to buildings, roads, bridges, etc., etc. If the Maharaja does not add to the public works, he should at least properly preserve what he has inherited from the past. Public works out of order, owing to want of repairs from time to time, always reflect disgrace on the Sarkar.

(*i*) Where the annual cost of repair is not likely to vary much, give permanent or standing sanctions for the repairs so that time and trouble may be saved and the necessary repairs may be executed in due season. For instance, such sanction may be given for the repair of the road from the City to the Camp and of the road from the City to Makkarpura.

(*i*) Give permanent sanctions for annual repairs.

(*j*) In repairing large and costly buildings, which have been built upon proper designs or after appropriate styles or in making any additions or alterations to such buildings, be careful not to act arbitrarily, be careful not to violate the original design or style. This is a mistake constantly committed in Native States.

(*j*) Do not spoil the original design.

(6) Public works such as Kutcherries, Court-houses, Jails, Schools, etc., etc., are indeed necessary to a civilized Government. But they are not, what are called, re-productive works—they are not works which directly increase the wealth of the people, but they are the most important and deserve special attention.

Public works deserve special attention.

(7) A Kutcherry is not a reproductive work because it does not add to the production of the country or diminish and save the expenditure of the

Promote all reproductive public works.

country. An irrigation well is a re-productive work, because it increases the crop of the land watered thereby. A road I consider to be a re-productive work, because it reduces and saves the cost of carrying goods. Earnestly, then, promote all re-productive public works. The more this is done, the better will it be for the country. The Gaekwar cannot conquer new territories, but it is in his power to increase the value of the territories already in his possession—to increase their value by means of re-productive public works.

Multiply wells and roads.

(8) The main thing in these territories is to arrange for the multiplication of irrigating wells and of useful roads.

Fair weather roads to be made.

(9) Fair weather roads should be made in abundance at a moderate cost per mile, so that ordinary country carts may move about easily in fair weather.

Metalled roads to be sparingly made.

(10). Metalled roads are very costly in the soil of Gujarat in consequence of the cost of procuring metal from a distance. Their annual maintenance is also very costly. Such roads have, therefore, to be very sparingly made—they should be made only where such high cost would be justifiable.

The best road is the rail-road.

(11) The best road for Gujarat is the little rail-road, such as already connects our town of Dabhoi with the city of Baroda, with Bahaderpur, with Chandode and with

Miagam. In the long run, it is really much cheaper than a metalled road, while it is infinitely more convenient. The advantages of a rail-road of the sort over a metalled road may be briefly stated as follows :—

(i) The cost of construction and repair is lower.

(ii) The charges for moving goods and passengers are clear.

(iii) The journey is performed much more comfortably and much more safely.

(iv) The journey may be performed in all seasons, irrespective of the state of the weather.

(v) The rail-road pays some return on the capital spent on the same, whereas a metalled road does not.

Multiply railways in Baroda.

(12) Therefore, the Government of Baroda ought to multiply such sorts of railway in its own territories wherever there is need for the same.

Repair tanks.

(13) In India generally, and in Gujarat specially, tanks and talaos are of great use to the people. The Public Works Department ought to keep such reservoirs in good repair.

Reclaim marshy tracts.

(14) The same department should undertake the reclamation of large marshy tracts for purposes of cultivation wherever this can be done at reasonable cost.

(15) Temples, Dharmshalas and such other public buildings should also have due attention in those instances in which their repair is the duty of the Sarkar.

Give attention to temples.

(16) In conclusion, let me say what perhaps it is needless to say—that it will undoubtedly be much better—infinitely better for the State to spend the surplus revenue on useful public works than adding to the already large stock of Palace jewellery. We have enough of personal ornaments. Let the country have its ornaments in the shape of useful public works. It is these that will raise the name and fame of the Maharaja.

Utilise surplus revenue on public works.

(17) As bearing on what I have just said, I feel tempted to read to Your Highness an eloquent passage from Edmund Burke, who was a great orator of the period of George III. I read this passage when I was a young man about to enter the world, but I vividly remember it to this day. Speaking on the irrigation works of a part of the Madras Presidency, Burke said :—

Burke on Irrigation Works.

" These are the monuments of real kings who were the fathers of their people ; testators to a posterity which they embraced as their own. These are the grand sepulchres built by ambition, but by the ambition of an insatiable benevolence which, not contented with reigning in the dispensation of happiness during the contracted term of human life, had strained, with all the reachings and graspings of a vivacious mind, to extend the dominion of their bounty beyond the limits of nature and to perpetuate themselves through generations of generations, the guardians, the protectors, the nourishers of mankind."

CHAPTER XXXIII.

EDUCATION

Wednesday, 20th July, 1881.

We set out by declaring that the first duty of the Government is to promote the happiness of the people. We have been considering various means by which the happiness of the people should be promoted. We have been chiefly considering the physical happiness of the people. It is now time to state that it is also the duty of the Government to look after the intellectual and moral advancement of the people. The origin of this duty is self-evident. The Maharaja is the father of his people, and the father wishes to make his children not only healthy and happy but wise also.

It is the duty of Government to look after the intellectual and moral advancement of the people.

(2) In India at least, it is evident that the State should take an active and leading part in the education of the people. If the State did nothing, the people themselves would do very little in the cause of public education.

The State to take an active part.

The Maharaja to improve existing conditions.

(3) What measures have been taken in the performance of this great duty of the government during these six years of the administration during Your Highness' minority, may be gathered in detail from the annual reports which have been printed and published. Your Highness will have not only to maintain the advance which has already been thus made, but to make further advances.

Some general principles.

(4) I will now place before Your Highness some general principles which have to be followed in the Educational Department of the State.

(*a*) English education to be placed within the reach of those disposed to acquire it.

(*a*) High Education through the medium of the English language, should be placed within the reach of those who are disposed to acquire the same. Those who have acquired high education through the medium of the English language will probably be the most enlightened members of the community. They will probably be the most effectual promoters of progress: they will probably be the foremost to correct the gross errors of ignorance and superstition. Indeed, my belief—my strong conviction—is that any Indian community in the present age would be stagnant without some such elements as just mentioned.

(b)The highest English School to be at the Capital.

(b) The highest and best English School should be at the Capital of the State, as it is. I hope, it will, before long, become one of the regular Colleges of India. We are providing it with a building which will do honor to Baroda.

(c) The Central School to have English professors.

(c) English literature, science and philosophy, are best taught by Englishmen. Therefore our Central Schools at the Capital should always have English gentlemen as professors. The temptation to appoint Natives for patriotical or economical motives should be firmly resisted. Natives, however, may answer well as Assistants to the English professors, especially in Mathematics and Natural Sciences.

(d) The number of Anglo-Vernacular schools to be increased.

(d) It is not enough to have one central school at the Capital as described above. Several feeders to the same should be established both at the Capital and in the Districts, in the shape of Anglo-Vernacular schools. The number we already have must be gradually increased.

(e)The scheme of studies to be the same as in English schools.

(e) The scheme of studies in all the above-mentioned schools should be the same as in corresponding British schools. The reason is this. If our scheme of studies were different, our youths would not be able to pass the Bombay University examinations; Our youths would not be able to get employment outside our territories. But it is highly desirable that we should so educate our youths as to enable them to find employment whether in our own territories or in the much larger field of British India.

(*f*) Let education make useful citizens.

(*f*) Though the scheme of studies is to be the same as in British India, I would urge our Professors to pay greater attention to the object of making our youths orderly and useful citizens. Cramming should be discouraged. The valuable faculty of thought and judgment should be better developed.

(*g*) No special religious instruction to be given.

(*g*) The education given should be mental in regard to religion; that is to say, no special religious instruction should be given.

(*h*) General morality to be taught.

(*h*) I would, however, strongly recommend that general and universal morality be taught in all our schools by means of a small and well-chosen tract. Similarly, let that morality be taught which the State enforces by pains and penalties—that morality which is embodied in the Penal Code. It seems to me quite essential that our youths should be taught early what motives, intentions, and acts are wrong and which of these are punishable by the State. Such teaching will not occupy more than a short time, but it will save many a youth from committing acts which are morally wrong or acts which are criminally punishable.

(*i*) The great mass of the people must be educated through the vernacular schools established at all centres of population including the Capital.

(*i*) The masses to be educated through the vernacular schools.

(*j*) The schools in the towns may well be entirely State schools. Those in the villages may be grant-in-aid schools. A judicious system of grants-in-aid will enable the State, at a comparatively small expense, to extensively control the education of the people.

(*j*) State schools in towns and grant-in-aid ones in the villages.

(*k*) The vernacular schools abovementioned include schools for girls wherever there is a demand for these.

(*k*) Schools for girls.

(*l*) There may be one central vernacular school at the Capital to impart high education. We already have one here known as the Vernacular College of Science. It has been tried as an experiment on the strong recommendation of such men as Rao Bahadur Vinayak Rao, Rao Bahadur Janardhan Gadgil, Dr. Bhalchandra and others. The experiment has, I am glad to say, proved a good success in several important respects. Further experience may suggest some modifications in its details, and may perhaps enable us to reduce its cost.

(*l*) One central vernacular school to impart high education.

(*m*) A special school for Eurasian children we already have at the Capital, and this must be kept up, of course.

(*m*) Special school for Eurasians.

(*n*) There are a few Sanskrit schools also ; and in a Native State, these are popular. Sanskrit learning must not be allowed to perish from neglect. But too many must not be tempted to become devotees to make a living by its means. I would prefer that Sanskrit schools should be in connection with and at the cost of well-endowed Hindu temples.

(*n*) Study of Sanskrit not to be neglected.

(*o*) At first at least, the school fees should be fixed low, so that education may be availed of to the largest extent. As education comes to be more valued—as the demand for it increases—the scale of fees may be raised gradually.

(*o*) The school fees to be low.

(5) The Maharaja should use his great influence to induce the Sirdars, Silladars, Darakdars, Sowkars, etc., etc., to send their children to school. As an example to these classes, the Maharaja should send to school the children of his own relations and friends.

Induce Sirdars and others to send their children to school.

(6) It should be remembered that education is much stimulated by giving educated men a decided preference in the exercise of patronage. In filling up vacancies in the various departments of the pub-

Prefer educated men in service.

lic service, the heads of departments should be directed to accord such preference consistently with the efficiency of the service.

Encourage higher study, by scholarships.

(7) Scholarships may be given to enable some of those who may have finished their course in our schools to prosecute their studies to a higher standard at Bombay or Poona, the scholarships being given to the deserving and on certain judicious conditions.

Preside at educational functions.

(8) His Highness the Maharaja should show his interest in education by personally presiding at the principal examinations or distribution of prizes, and by making encouraging addresses. This is one of His Highness' public duties.

Encourage Libraries.

(9) Public Libraries, Reading Rooms, Lectures and all other similar educational agencies should be assisted and encouraged.

Improve the moral tone, by personal example.

(10) By steadily acting on the main lines above suggested, the intellectual and moral welfare of the people will be gradually but effectually promoted and one of the most important duties of the State will be fulfilled. His Highness the Maharaja, being the highest and most powerful personage in the country, may do much to improve the moral tone of the people. The Maharaja's example must operate

daily and hourly. His Highness' very conversation will be pregnant with results.

Encourage virtue and check vice.

(11) It is, therefore, most desirable that His Highness the Maharaja should avail himself of the numerous occasions which will often occur, to make known his love of virtue and his aversion to vice. He may easily do this by throwing out remarks as each occasion may suggest. For instance, His Highness may say, " I do not at all like those who speak untruths," or " I hate public servants who take bribes," or " I have a great contempt for talebearers," or " Let no one suppose that he will prosper by intrigues," or " If a man breaks the law he must suffer for it," and so forth. The same remarks may be varied thus, " I esteem those who are truthful," " I am much pleased with honest public servants," and so on. Be sure that numbers of people will closely watch such remarks falling from the Maharaja and will disseminate them far and wide. Every such remark will produce a most salutary effect. It will encourage good people, and it will reform bad people. It will warn all. Indeed I think that the Maharaja may thus become a powerful teacher. He may, in a few years, acquire the glory of improving the general moral tone. And let it be remembered that the more the general tone is improved, the easier and the better will government become and the greater will be the

happiness of the people. In short, it is one great duty of the Maharaja to employ his authority and influence to encourage virtue, and to check vice. His words, his deeds, the distribution of his favours, the bestowal of appointments and honours must all be directed to that great and beneficial end.

CHAPTER XXXIV.

THE PALACE DEPARTMENT.

27th July, 1881.

An important Department.

I wish to speak to-day about the Palace. This is a very important Department, because it is the personal establishment of His Highness the Maharaja, the Ruler of the State. The main objects, with reference to which Palace affairs are to be arranged and managed, are to make the Maharaja and his family perfectly comfortable and happy and to enable them to maintain the requisite degree of state in the eyes of the people.

The high expenditure necessary to maintain the pomp.

(2) Whatever expenditure is necessary for these purposes must, of course, be incurred and is quite justifiable. This expenditure must be higher in an Asiatic State than in a European State, because of the difference of circumstances, and of the difference of habits, customs and feelings. An Indian community has been for ages, accustomed to associate a great deal of pomp and show with the possession of power. In fact, the people estimate power by the display of wealth that accompanies it.

(3) At the same time, it is clear that the Palace expenditure should bear a reasonable proportion to the income of the State. If it exceeds the reasonable proportion, what follows? The sources of the State for promoting the happiness of the people get diminished. In other words, a certain part of the happiness of the people is sacrified. It has to be remembered that the first duty of the ruler is to make his people as happy as possible.

But it should be reasonable.

(4) What the reasonable proportion which the Palace expenditure should bear to the income of a State like Baroda is, cannot be so precisely determined as to command the assent of everybody, still it cannot be left altogether an indeterminate quantity. My own common sense, assisted by my experience, leads me to think that in the existing circumstances the annual Palace expenditure should not ordinarily exceed 10 (ten) per cent. of the income of the State, that is to say, one-tenth of the income.

It should not exceed one tenth of the revenue.

(5) It is exceedingly desirable for the Maharaja to fix for himself the reasonable proportion and to command the Palace authorities concerned to keep the expenditure within that proportion. Those authorities must be made with a strong will to obey the Maharaja's commands in this important respect. If His Highness is really earnest in the

Fix the reasonable proportion.

matter, he will find no difficulty in adhering to the limit.

Fix a Budget for each sub-department.

(6) Each sub-department of the Palace should have a Budget or scale of expenditure prescribed and the Maharaja should insist on this being addressed. The great principle is to leave as few items as possible undefined; for, leave any item undefined, and it will be found that that item has a great tendency to grow from year to year.

Reserve the power of giving special sanctions.

(7) But there must be some few items which, from their nature, cannot admit of being defined. Such items should be kept under control by the Maharaja, preserving for himself the power of giving special sanctions from time to time.

There should be a distinct Treasury for the Palace.

(8) There should always be a distinct Treasury for the Palace. It should draw the appointed funds from time to time from the Public Central Treasury. There should be no confusion of these two Treasuries. Every item of Palace income and of Palace expenditure should be credited and debited respectively to the Palace Treasury, so that the accounts of this Treasury may afford a complete view of the Palace receipts and expenditure.

Orders to be given in writing.

(9) In money matters let the orders be given as much as possible in writing. Oral orders are very slippery and unsafe,

and after the lapse of time cause all sorts of doubts and difficulties. Written orders are especially necessary where unusual or special or large expenditure is concerned.

Salaries to be regularly disbursed.

(10) See that salaries and other payments are regularly and promptly disbursed. This will be a great boon to a large number of servants, small and great and also to tradesmen, etc.

Loans from the Treasury to be avoided.

(11) Loans of money from the Palace Treasury should be totally avoided. The Palace Treasury is not to be a Bank. Great firmness is required in maintaining this principle; otherwise, a most pernicious and wasteful system would spring up.

Salary of six months may be advanced.

(12) The utmost assistance which may be given to a deserving palace servant is to accommodate him with an advance of salary or allowance for a period not exceeding 6 months or at most one year. His Highness' special sanction should be made necessary for giving any such advance, and such advances should be strictly recovered at the appointed time.

A reliable Head Accountant to be in charge of accounts.

(13) A thoroughly competent and reliable Head Accountant should be made responsible to keep the Palace Accounts regularly and systematically. All tendency to laxity and delay should be firmly

checked. Every expenditure should be immediately brought to account. To the utmost extent possible, the year's account should include every expenditure incurred in the year. In other words, avoid the expenditure of a given year being charged to some future year. It is thus alone that the expenditure of one year can be fairly and usefully compared with the expenditure of another year.

Audit of accounts.

(14) The regular audit of the Palace Accounts by the Huzur Auditor must be well maintained; otherwise, there would be little or no practical check, and all would slide into confusion.

No private expenditure from the Public Treasury.

(15) No private expenditure of the Maharaja, that is to say, no expenditure which properly belongs to the Palace, should be ordered from or transferred to the Public Treasury. This used to be done largely before, for the purpose of showing less expenditure at the Palace. It was a fraudulent system which should never be revived.

Do not increase expenditure arbitrarily.

(16) As a general rule, the expenditure in any particular item should not be increased unless there are funds available from savings elsewhere. Let increase here be balanced by decrease there. This simple principle being steadily kept in view and acted on, the aggregate Palace expenditure will be generally maintained at its usual level. *Example:*—

A *chobdar* begs for some increase of pay. Let it not be granted blindly. There are lots of *chobdars*. When a vacancy occurs, either abolish the post or reduce the pay of the post, and thus find funds for increasing the pay of the *chobdar* concerned. In short, when any increase is to be given, inquire what disengaged funds are available for it and give the increase out of such funds. For this purpose, the Palace Head Accountant should be consulted on such occasions, and he should be directed to keep His Highness informed of the progress of the expenditure.

Examination of the Treasury balances every month by officials.

(17) A monthly examination of the balances in the Palace Treasury is most necessary. Two or three of the principal officials of the Palace should make such examination personally and certify to His Highness in a memo, under their signature that the balances stood at such a figure and tallied with the accounts. These memoranda should be regularly entered in a book, and the book itself should be preserved as a record.

Consider past dakhlas.

(18) Priests, astrologers and other persons of such class are ever desirous of increasing the expenditure and need to be kept under close control. They should be considerately treated, but must not be allowed to transgress their limits. The best method of effecting this object is to lay hold of

past moderate *dakhlas* (precedents) and to insist upon these not being exceeded.

Tendency of the ladies to increase expenditure.

(19) The ladies of the Palace care nothing about public finances, and have a great tendency to propose increased expenditure constantly in one way or another. Here, too, past moderate *dakhlas* must be availed of to restrain the tendency. *Dakhlas* are much respected in Native States, and an appeal to *dakhlas* is generally conclusive. By appealing to *dakhlas* a great deal of personal unpleasantness is avoided.

Banks in the name of ladies.

(20) The former practice of opening *dookans* or banks in the name and on behalf of these ladies, and of other relations and friends, was an exceedingly pernicious one. It has been totally discontinued and must, on no account, be revived.

The Palace not to assist the ladies in their private debts.

(21) These ladies and indeed all others concerned should be made to understand clearly that the Palace will not assist them in regard to any private debts they may incur. Indeed, they must not incur such debts, and if they do, they must themselves pay the debts off from their allowances.

The evil of accumulating hoards.

(22) The Maharaja should never and need never think of accumulating hoards in the Palace as personal funds. Any desire on the part of His Highness to make

private hoards must lead him much astray. There are many sad instances showing that such desire has led to the greatest public evils.

Reduce wasteful expenditure.

(23) There is much needless, useless, or wasteful expenditure in the Palace, which the Maharaja may well reduce. It contributes neither to His Highness' comfort and happiness nor to His Highness' dignity and state. The funds thus disengaged would more than suffice for making needed improvements and for supplying existing deficiencies. Reductions and retrenchments, however, should be so made as not to cause any sudden or serious hardships to individuals.

The 'Kothi' to be properly managed.

(24) The *Kothi* branch of the Palace should be conquered and subjugated by the firmness of the Maharaja. It has been a stronghold of irregularities and abuses. Its existing condition and working should be carefully examined. Some things may be immediately rectified and others gradually according to opportunities afforded by changes and vacancies.

New 'Sidhas' to be ordered by the Maharaja in writing.

(25) No one except the Maharaja himself should have the power of ordering the issue of new *sidhas*; and when His Highness himself orders any such, it is essential that the order should be in writing, and also that the orders should distinctly specify the time for which the *sidhas* are to run.

This precaution is so necessary because the most temporary issues of *sidhas* have often run on for years and have become ever hereditary !

Don't add to the religious expenditure.

(26) Religious and charitable expenditure is already very large. Every care has to be exercised to prevent fresh additions to it. Readjustments may be made if necessary or desirable.

The practice of granting, 'vershasans' not to be revived.

(27) The reckless practice of granting *Vershasans* should not be revived. If rarely granted in special cases, the amount should be moderate ; it should come out of some saving caused by a vacancy. It should not go beyond the life of the grantee.

Daksina and Dans.

(28) The *Shravana Daksina, Bidaji Ramnah,* and such other items have a very great tendency to break loose from control. Certain limits have now-a-days been fixed for these, and the Maharaja's firmness may well be shown in compelling adherence to these salutary limits. There are many *dans*—such as *go-dans*, etc., which are repeatedly given by the Maharaja and other members of the Gaekwar family. I apprehend that many abuses have crept in this direction. It is desirable for His Highness to give some attention to these matters and make these many and costly *dans* subservient to really useful ends—such as the encouragement of learning or the relief of penury and distress.

CHAPTER XXXV.

THE PALACE DEPARTMENT—(*contd.*)

3rd August, 1881.

Guard against Mis-appropriation.

There is probably some theft, misappropriation, abuse, and waste going on still in different branches of the Palace, though much, no doubt, has been reduced under the eye of Her Highness the Maharani Jamnabai Saheb. The Maharaja may, under proper arrangement, be able to minimise those things.

The jewellery requires special attention.

(2) There is a very large and costly stock of jewellery in the Palace, which will require the special and early attention of the Maharaja—there is much of gold and silver things also to be looked after. Lists of the foregoing have been made, and copies are available in the Palace and Fadnavis *Daftars*. It is very desirable that the Maharaja should go over the whole stock and become personally acquainted with what there is. His Highness' personal inspection will have its moral effects.

Its periodical examination by a Committee.

(3) The whole stock being once clearly gone over by the Maharaja himself personally, arrangements should be made for a regular periodical exami-

nation of the stock by a trustworthy Committee, who should certify to His Highness in writing that it is all right. The Committee should see also to the identity of the precious stones, pearls, etc., which are liable to be changed.

Jewellery to be in the custody of responsible persons.

(4) The whole should be in custody of trustworthy and responsible persons. One official would hardly suffice, for he might fall sick, or have to go on leave or even die. I would suggest a sort of Committee composed of persons who have sufficient allowances property, etc., etc. In short, there should be sufficient security against loss.

Iron-room for jewellery.

(5) Formerly the jewellery, etc., used to be placed in miserable little dark rooms and scattered about. Everything was very loosely managed. Now, however, the main stock is placed in a strong iron-room which contains separate boxes, but which is under one lock. This is a safe and convenient arrangement in many respects, and ought, I think, to be by all means continued.

Excessive presents from the stock to be avoided.

(6) This being an inherited stock of very valuable property, the Maharaja may well be proud of maintaining it. Therefore, needless or large or excessive presents from the same should be avoided. When, however, some presents become necessary, the minor items may be used.

(7) It suggests itself as a good plan to divide the things into those which are for the personal use of the Maharaja, those for Maharani, and so on. The rest will go under the head of "miscellaneous," and may be available for presents, etc., when presents become necessary.

Jewellery to be arranged under different heads.

(8) It is of the utmost importance that the accounts of the jewel *khana* should be kept with the greatest regularity, punctuality, and strictness. The Chief Palace authorities should be held fully responsible for this. I mean accounts of stocks, of presents, of loans for use, of changes made by breaking up one ornament and making another, and so forth. The accounts should be written in regular bound books, not in loose pages, not even in loosely bound *chopdas*. The accounts should bear the signatures of the writing karkoon and of the immediately responsible officials, and should be countersigned or initialled by one of the Chief Officers of the Palace.

Accounts to be kept with care.

(9) Formerly there used to be a bad system of lending the jewellery, etc., for the use of various persons. It led to many and grave abuses and loss. I have had many instances before me, in which jewellery merely given on loan has been retained or claimed as gifts. Loans should therefore, be as

Loans from jewellery to be very sparing.

sparing as possible. When made, they must be made under the sanction of the Maharaja. Every loan should be entered unmistakably as a loan. Receipts should be taken from those to whom the loan is made. The loan should be expressly stated to be for a certain period, at the end of which the things should be replaced. Responsibility in all these respects should be clearly defined and strictly enforced. Unless these and other careful and strict arrangements are made, laxity and loss are pretty sure to ensue. Property has its trouble in taking care of it!

Further investments in jewellery not desirable.

(10) I would strongly advise His Highness against any further investments in jewellery and plate. What there is already in hand is really much more than sufficient for the largest and the most ambitious Royal family. If any new ornaments are ever required, they may well be made out of the materials available in the jewel-room. If there are rough ornaments, they may easily be converted into elegant ones. It would be unwise to leave unused a lot of costly ornaments and to make new purchases, and thereby needlessly swell the Palace expenditure.

Resist the temptations offered by jewellers.

(11) I would warn the Maharaja against the many temptations which jewellers are sure to offer to make new purchases. They will show their ornaments

in fine new cases to the ladies and induce them by various arts to press His Highness to purchase them. They will not hesitate even to bribe those who may have influence with the ladies. Such temptations will have to be firmly resisted. It is a matter which furnishes abundant scope for the exercise of the virtue of firmness. The ladies may often be assured that similar ornaments are already in the Palace-stock, or that similar ornaments may be made out of the stock in a very short time.

"Janghur" not to be revived.

(12) What is known as *janghur* has been discontinued and should by no means be revived. By *janghur* is meant a number of ornaments brought by jewellers and left at the Palace for purchase by His Highness as opportunities occur. It has been a source of the most troublesome disputes. The jeweller contends that his ornaments are actually purchased, whereas they were kept only on inspection. Then disputes arise about prices and payments—matters, in themselves complicated by crafty men at the Palace inducing the ladies to use ornaments not yet purchased! Such troubles and complications are best avoided by making it a rule not to take any ornaments from a jeweller until after the price has been settled and the purchase has been made. This is a simple rule.

(13) To proceed to other matters. The carriages, horses, and other equipments of the Palace have not been in the best order. The Maharaja may greatly improve these without material increase of expenditure. The general rule should be that whatever His Highness personally uses should be of the best description. For it is better to have ten good carriages than twenty bad ones. This principle applies to a great number of matters connected with the Palace. I will here give just one more instance. The personal attendants of the Maharaja should be well chosen and well-dressed men, which they hardly are at present.

Carriages, etc., to be the best, and personal attendants to be well dressed.

(14) The Palace gardens cost annually very large sums of money and yet scarcely any garden is what it ought to be in beauty, or production. There is room for considerable improvement in this direction.

Improve the palace gardens.

(15) The sanitary condition of the Palace, though somewhat improved of late, is yet far from what it might be. Too many servants live in the Palace, and they are allowed to live in the most dirty manner.

Improve sanitation.

(16) A great number of rare or curious things have been, from time to time, purchased by the Gaekwar, but they are lying scattered about the Palace. It is desirable to collect and arrange them at one

Arrange rare or curious things.

convenient place, so that the Maharaja may know what things exist, and put them to use.

Punctuality in Durbars.

(17) Greater punctuality may be observed in regard to Palace Durbars, ceremonies, etc. All concerned, being once or twice duly warned, will attend at the appointed hour, and time will thus be saved and convenience promoted.

Order of precedence in Durbars not to be disturbed.

(18) A certain order of precedence is now observed at these Durbars and in State Processions. For the sake of peace, this order should be strictly maintained, and no change should be made unless found to be clearly necessary. There is great ambition and great rivalry in these matters. Several Durbaris will come, and entreat and press His Highness to give them higher seats, etc., and will adduce the most abundant arguments. But His Highness will find it the best course to meet all such solicitations by saying, "I must adhere to the existing order and arrangements, and can make no change unless I am convinced that a change is absolutely necessary." If changes were lightly or incautiously made, much disturbance of feeling, much heartburning, and many troubles and embarrassments would be sure to arise and continue a long time. If, however, any change must be considered, the Maharaja would do well to appoint a committe and to direct it to enquire

into the matter and submit their opinion to His Highness. Such a committee should include the representatives of the various sections of the Durbar, such as a Sirdar, a Darakdar, a Mankari, etc., etc. The head of the Military Department of the Huzur Cutcherry may also be associated in the inquiry. On the Committee reporting on the matter, His Highness may consider and dispose of the same. The Dewan may well be consulted also with advantage. The great principles to be kept in view in dealing with such matters, are, first, to make as few changes as possible in the existing arrangements and secondly to make no such change as would disturb the feelings of many Durbaris.

A diary for recording daily events.

(19) It is very desirable to arrange that a regular diary be kept in the Palace, fully recording the particulars of daily occurrences. Everything worth remembering should be entered therein. Such a record will be exceedingly useful for various purposes, and especially for preserving precedents for future guidance.

Proper organisation of the Palace is wanted.

(20) The foregoing enumeration of important points will be of use to His Highness when he assumes the management of the Palace and its appurtenances. His Highness will also have some idea of how much requires attention and arrangement. The work to be done is immense, and it is clear that His High-

ness alone cannot do it. What is required is proper organization in the Palace. The work and responsibility should be appropriately distributed. The servants should be grouped and placed under superior officials. These superior officials should have certain powers, and the subordinates must be made to obey their superiors. Otherwise, business would not go on properly. The Maharaja cannot himself see that every servant duly attends and does his allotted work. He cannot himself grant leave of absence to every servant from the *bhangee* to the *Kamdar*. He cannot himself appoint and dismiss punkah-pullers, gardeners, mahouts, etc., etc.

The Kamdar, with sufficient powers to be at the head.

(21) At the head of the whole, and immediately under the orders of His Highness, should be the Palace *Kamdar*. He should be a high officer of capacity and integrity, not much inferior in these respects to the head of any department in the Huzur Cutcherry. He should be given sufficient powers * for the conduct of ordinary business—I mean certain limited powers for appointing, dismissing, fining, granting leave, etc., and for incurring ordinary expenditure. He should be well supported by His Highness in the exercise of his legitimate powers and influences.

---

* NOTE.—The Palace authorities, however, exercise no civil or criminal jurisdiction. Cases falling under such jurisdiction shall be transferred by them to the constituted authorities of the State.

Annual Administration report to be prepared.

(22) At the end of each official year, the Palace *Kamdar* should be directed to prepare and submit to His Highness a full report of the Palace Administration, together with statistics and explanations. This report will be of great use to His Highness in controlling Palace affairs.

CHAPTER XXXVI

HUZUR CUTCHERRY

10th August, 1881.

The Maharaja as the Ruler, represents the power of the State, and the Huzur Cutcherry is the machinery kept in motion by that power. The whole in effect constitutes the Government of the country responsible to promote the welfare of the people.

What constitutes the government.

(2) The Huzur Cutcherry should therefore, be intellectually and morally strong. This is a most essential condition of successful administration by the Maharaja. The more that Cutcherry is strong intellectually and morally, the more will it be a credit and comfort to the Maharaja, and the more will it command the respect of the people.

The essential condition of administration.

(3) The Dewan being at the head of the Huzur Cutcherry, he ought to be, as near as possible, the ideal of a Dewan. In point of capacity and probity, he should deserve and possess the confidence of the Maharaja. He (the Dewan) should also deserve and possess the respect of the British Government.

The ideal of a Dewan.

He should be a person who has had experience in the work of administration. Better if this experience has, partly at least, been in administering a Native State. Still better, if the experience has been gained in the service of the Baroda State itself.

Choose your Dewan from the Cutcherry.

(4) These are very important considerations which must be kept fully in view by the Maharaja in selecting his Dewan. They point clearly to the desirableness of so arranging that there may always be some men of the requisite capacity and character in the Huzur Cutcherry itself and trained in the work of Administration. It will be best to choose the Dewan from such men.

i. e. from the Heads of Departments.

(5) It is the special interest of the Maharaja to have such men for the heads of the department of the Huzur Cutcherry as may, in time, be fit to be promoted to the Dewanship. In looking after the interests of the Maharaja during His Highness' minority, I am glad that this important principle has by no means been overlooked. At this moment, there are such men in the Huzur Cutcherry.

Importing an outsider not very desirable.

(6) If the policy above indicated were not adopted and followed, the Maharaja would be in great embarrassment whenever the Dewan's post becomes vacant. Not finding suitable men in His Highness'

own service, His Highness would have to import some outsider—a course certainly attended with much risk and with many disadvantages.

Reasons.

(7) It can seldom be comfortable to the Maharaja to have a perfect stranger as Dewan—one with whom he has had no previous intercourse—one whose temper and ways are unknown to him—one who does not know the country and people—one who is unacquainted with the principles and details of the local Administration—one who perhaps may depend for support on external powers or influences more than on His Highness himself. More might be said on this part of the subject, but probably it would be needless, for the Maharaja can easily realize the disadvantages of bringing in a stranger as his Dewan.

Qualifications of a Dewan.

(8) To pursue the qualities necessary in a Dewan of His Highness, he should of course, be well versed in the English language. Without this, no Dewan of such a large State as Baroda would get on at all usefully even for a short time. He should be a warm friend and well-wisher of Native States. As such he should always be ready to do his best to protect and preserve the Native State and all its legitimate rights and privileges. He should be firm yet conciliatory, just yet mild and merciful,

energetic yet patient and considerate, zealous yet discreet and circumspect, sensitive to honour yet by no means quarrelsome, agreeable to the Maharaja yet free and frank in giving sound advice. He should be a friend of progressive improvement in all branches of the Administration, yet he should possess discrimination enough to conserve what is old, natural, and useful.

The Maharaja to cordially support the Dewan.

(9) Having most carefully selected the right person as his Dewan, the Maharaja should give him his cordial support and encouragement.

Bad policy of changing the Dewan at short intervals.

(10) It would be very bad policy for the Maharaja to change his Dewan at short intervals, without strong reasons. A Dewan should have the fair prospect of holding his office at least for five years. It is only a sign of weakness in a Maharaja to change his Chief Minister frequently, and thus to interrupt useful service.

Heads of departments to be carefully selected.

(11) We may pass on to the heads of departments under the Dewan. These also need to be very carefully selected. They should be quite qualified to perform well the important duties entrusted to them, and they should afford a fair promise of being trained, so as to undertake the duties of Chief Minister, if at any time required. It follows that the heads of departments should be selected for

qualifications similar to those which the Dewan himself should possess.

They should know English.

(12) As a rule, the heads of departments should be conversant with English. The only exception to this that may be tolerated, is the Fadnis.

Diversity of castes desirable.

(13) Some diversity of castes and creeds in these heads of departments is desirable. Indeed, it is desirable throughout the public service.

The heads to co-operate with the Dewan.

(14) The heads of departments should cordially co-operate with the Dewan in the work of good government. All being men of high character and principles, there should be nothing like intriguing or factious oppositions. The Maharaja and the Dewan should have every reason to feel that these departmental heads render loyal assistance at all times. The expectations of the Maharaja in this respect should be clearly and decidedly made known.

Important matters to be discussed by all the Ministers.

(15) These departmental heads are, in fact, the several departmental ministers of the Maharaja, and the Dewan is the chief or Prime Minister. The whole is the cabinet of the Maharaja. The ordinary business of each department may be conducted by its head under the orders or supervision of the Dewan. But, if any business of considerable

importance or difficulty is to be done, all or most of the ministers should meet, discuss, and decide. Should any serious differences of opinion arise, His Highness the Maharaja will do well to patiently hear the opinion and arguments of each of his ministers. How His Highness himself should decide in such a situation, I have indicated under the head of Minor Hints.

Ministers to be treated with confidence.

(16) All the ministers should be treated with consideration and confidence. Credit should be fully and even liberally given to each for the good administration of his particular department. An occasional expression of deserved praise by the Maharaja is sure to have an encouraging effect beyond any amount of money rewards, for honourable men are ambitious of honour and fame. In short, each minister should be made to feel it to be his interest, pleasure and pride to have his department in the best order, and thereby to contribute to the high reputation of the whole administration of His Highness the Maharaja.

Their trivial errors may be passed over.

(17) It should be remembered that even the best of men are liable to err. Men who are continually acting must make errors to a certain extent. Trivial errors, such as are the common lot of humanity, should not be made too much of in these ministers. Such trivial errors may be altogether passed over

by the Maharaja, or, if they must be noticed, let them be lightly noticed.

Censure to be in moderate terms.

(18) A serious error, however, may be sometimes committed, and may require a regular censure. Even then, the censure should be in carefully measured and moderate terms. It should be reluctantly dealt out. It should not cause more pain than absolutely necessary in the public interests. Therefore the sensitiveness and self-respect of the person to be censured should be fully taken into account. And the justice of the censure may be enhanced by a judicious mixture of deserved praise. The right dispensation of censure is a little science and art in itself.

Let the minister explain.

(19) In this connection, it should be remembered that it would not be just or judicious to pass any censure on any minister before hearing what he has to say in defence or explanation of that part of his conduct which appears questionable.

Avoid the tone of peremptory command.

(20) All the ministers are, of course, the servants of the Maharaja, yet a wise Maharaja will avoid the use of the terms and tone of peremptory command. It is avoided by noble natures even in dealing with common menial servants. It is not necessary because the wishes of His Highness will carry weight of their own.

Organisation and discipline extremely necessary for successful administration.

(21) The Huzur Cutcherry is a large establishment. In it, therefore, and indeed in the public service generally, organization and discipline are extremely necessary for successful administration. In Native States, however, there is too great and constant a tendency to relax, and even to destroy organization and discipline—a tendency which the Maharaja has, therefore, to be all the more careful to resist. Organization, roughly speaking, means the proper division and distribution of work; making certain officials do the work assigned and holding them responsible for the proper performance of the aforesaid work, and placing under their orders the necessary hands for doing that work. The work is thus divided from top to bottom. Every portion of the work is entrusted to some responsible official, and every official from the lowest karkoon to the minister is placed immediately under the orders of some superior officer. Such organization, then, embraces the whole establishment and makes the whole establishment one organized body or one machine, each part of which works in subordination to some other part. And discipline, roughly speaking, means the enforcing of such subordination in all its gradations. It is thus and thus alone, that large bodies of men can be made to direct all their consistent energies to the accom-

plishment of great and complex ends. Without organization and discipline there is sure to be confusion. There will be little or nothing to compel each man to act in constant reference to the common end. Men will not only not act in concert but they may act so as to counteract each other. Much power will thus be actually wasted. Organization and discipline make a very great difference in the effectiveness of a body of men. This is most prominently exemplified by an army with the advantage of organization and discipline as compared with an equal army not possessing that advantage. The former will most easily beat the latter. Indian History shows repeated instances of immense numbers of unorganized and undisciplined forces being put to flight by a very small but efficiently organized and disciplined force.

Illustrations to show the importance of discipline.

(22) The Maharaja, I repeat, should fully maintain organization and discipline in his service. Official A, who is placed under the orders of official B, will come and say to His Highness, "I do not like to be under the orders of official B, I prefer to be directly under the orders of Your Highness, or at least under the orders of the Dewan." This should by no means be permitted. Again, a Subha, instead of obtaining leave of absence from his immediate superior, makes a direct application to the Maharaja. The Maharaja should return such

application and tell the applicant that he has acted irregularly and direct that he should apply to his immediate superior. He pleads that he did so because the Bai Saheb wanted him in connection with some business. The Maharaja should not allow this, but have the conduct of the officer duly noticed. Again, a karkoon rushes up to His Highness and complains that the Subha has unjustly fined him. The karkoon should be directed to represent the matter to the Huzur Cutcherry. Again, a Sardar calls upon His Highness and complains that the Zilla Judge has made a decree which is quite unjust, and that the Sardar requests that His Highness himself, or at least the Dewan, may call for the decree and revise it. The Sardar should be directed to appeal to the Varisht Court. Again, a jeweller comes up to His Highness and says, "Mr. Vinayek Rao has decided my case very unjustly. Let Kazi Saheb examine my case and decide again." Similarly, a ryot comes up to His Highness and says, "Kazi Saheb has assessed my lands very high. Let Raoji Vithal call for and examine my papers, and I am sure justice will be done to me." Similarly, a Public Works Contractor comes up to His Highness and represents: "The Engineer unjustly refuses to give me a certain work on contract. I pray that Mr. Pestonji may be directed to look into the matter and to do me justice." And so forth. Such applications are very common in Native States, because of the lack or deficiency of organization and discipline. Now, if such applications were complied with by an easy-going and thoughtless Maharaja, what would be the inevitable consequence? Surely, the greatest confusion of work and responsibility. There would be an end of all organization and discipline. Misgovernment could not but follow.

Each Minister to have powers.

(23) To enable each minister of His Highness to administer his allotted department efficiently, he should have powers to punish or reward within certain limits as respects his own subordinates. So long as he exercises these powers fairly, he should be strongly supported.

Petitions against ministers how to be dealt with.

(24) In Native States, the most false or reckless imputations are often made in petitions against the ministers. The ministers, being honourable men, such petitions require to be dealt with, with the utmost caution and discrimination.

Anonymous and vague petitions.

(25) As a general rule, anonymous petitions, or petitions bearing fictitious names, should be left unnoticed. Similarly, petitions which make vague and general imputations should also be left unnoticed.

Specific charges may be examined.

(26) When a petition comes from a known person and contains clear and specific charges affecting the minister's public conduct, the matter may possibly

require some consideration. The writer may have to be sent for and questioned as to the sources of his information, as to what evidence he is in a position to offer, as to the particular motives he may be actuated by, and so forth. What may be elicited from him will have to be judged as to probability or improbability in reference to the high character of the public officer concerned. After all this, some correct decision may be taken as to the course to be adopted. I would recommend to the Maharaja that he should refer such petitions to the Dewan who will, after due consideration and consultation, submit his best advice for His Highness' consideration.

The public to know that the ministers enjoy the ruler's confidence.

(27) The Dewan and the departmental ministers being chosen as suggested, not only should they actually enjoy the confidence and support of the Maharaja, but it should be made known to the public that they enjoy His Highness' confidence and support, for any supposition or suspicion to the contrary on the part of the public would be sure to lead to innumerable intrigues and would weaken the whole administration and injure the interests of the country.

How it can be made known to the public.

(28) The question here arises as to how that fact is to be made known to the public. The Maharaja may effect this end in many ways. For instance,

by His Highness generally accepting the opinions and the statements of his ministers, by treating these with consideration and friendly feelings, by occasionally speaking of them in favourable terms, by checking those who recklessly blame them; by refusing to join in the expression of pleasure by petty or thoughtless men at violent and groundless attacks on the ministry, and so on.

The minister's influence not to be weakened in the eyes of the public.

(29) Even when a minister has done something which needs to be cancelled or reversed, the necessary action should generally be so taken as not to shake or weaken the authority and influence of that Minister in the eyes of the public. For example—suppose a minister has dismissed a karkoon or other official without sufficient reason, and that it is desired to restore that karkoon. In such a case, it would not be necessary to make any fuss about it. It would not be necessary to record a formal order that the said dismissal was wrong and that the karkoon should be reinstalled. It would generally be sufficient to speak quietly to the minister and ask him to restore the karkoon quietly. It is in this spirit, as far as possible, that such business should be done.

Differences to be adjusted privately.

(30) In short, the Maharaja and his chosen ministers should be, and should also appear, as one and not as divided among themselves. Any differences

which might arise among them should be adjusted confidentially and should not be exposed to the public view.

Bad policy to make the ministers fight against each other.

(31) After what I have said, it would be quite needless for me to point out the bad policy—the very bad policy of making the ministers fight among themselves as a check against each other. It would be a very clumsy check, indeed, and applicable only if the Ministers were a set of bad, unprincipled persons. But by hypothesis, the Maharaja has chosen good ministers. By all means, let thieves quarrel among themselves, but not good men.

Rather, prevent quarrels.

(32) On the contrary, I say it is one of the most important duties of the Maharaja to prevent quarrels among his ministers, His Highness should occasionally express pleasure when his ministers work harmoniously together, and express or indicate displeasure when discord makes its appearance among them. Again, whenever the Maharaja sees that any intriguers or others try to break the harmony prevailing among His Highness' ministers and try to bring about quarrels among them, His Highness should firmly check such attempts.

How to promote harmony among the ministers.

(33) One great means of promoting harmony among the ministers and of making them collectively responsible for good adminstration is to arrange that each

Minister should discuss with his colleagues every matter of great public importance or difficulty which he has to deal with, and come to a common agreement about the course to be pursued. In this way, every matter of importance will have the benefit of discussion, and all the ministers will be responsible for the action of each. No minister will have it in his power to say that another minister has done wrong. Indeed, the chances of wrong action will be reduced to a minimum, and this is exactly what good administration requires.

The continuity of useful practical knowledge.

(34) Another advantage of great value accruing from the principle I have just stated is this: As each minister discusses important departmental matters with the other ministers, every minister becomes acquainted, not simply with the business of his own department, but with the important business of all departments. Such being the case, should any minister happen to go away, there would be no gap of knowledge in the ministry on that account. The successor of the last minister will soon be trained to his work by the other ministers. Thus the continuity of useful practical knowledge will be provided for.

CHAPTER XXXVII

HEADS OF DEPARTMENTS

Wednesday, 24th August, 1881

A few observations on the Heads of departments.

I have pointed out the great importance of the Huzur Cutcherry being made as strong as possible intellectually and morally as the essental condition of His Highness' successful administration. And I have indicated in general terms what sort of men the Dewan and the Heads of departments should be. I will now offer some further observations regarding these Heads of departments.

Qualifications of the Head of the Revenue Department.

(2) The Head of the Revenue Department should be specially conversant with the principles and details of his work. He must know all about the ryotwari system of land revenue. He must know all about Opium, Abkari, Customs, and other sources of revenue. In respect of all these matters, he must know, (1) the past history of each, (2) its present condition, (3) its condition in British India, and (4) its theory or science as enumerated by the best authorities. He must be versed in Finance generally. He must be familiar with Political Economy. It is only then that he will be able to do justice to the important department of Revenue, on which the happiness of the people largely depends.

Why the Heads under the former regimé were not successful.

(3) Those who were at the head of this department under the former regime mostly fell short of this standard. Not knowing the English language, they had no access to valuable and necessary information. Their chief idea was that the largest possible revenue should be extracted from the people with the least trouble to themselves. What was the consequence ? The interest of the people suffered more or less materially. Here there was excessive and crushing taxation. There the taxation was unequal. Here taxation was accompanied by oppression and vexation. There it was attended with the greatest vagueness and uncertainty. Every *Izardar* imposed or increased taxes at his own pleasure. The extent to which trade suffered from unprincipled duties and from the most extensively mischievous net-work of *nakahs* cannot be adequately imagined by the superficial observer. Many other instances of mismanagement might be mentioned here if he had time to do so. The fact is, those who were at the heads of departments in former times did not even know that great evils existed. How could they then think of improvement ?

The Revenue Department to be properly managed.

(4) It may be remembered in this connection that this department constantly comes in contact with hundreds of thousands of people. These will

be in a reasonable state of contentment if the Department is properly managed. If not properly managed, great will be the outcry.

The Head of the Judicial Department to be a lawyer.

(5) To proceed to other Departments of the Huzur Cutcherry. The Head of the Judicial, Police and Extradition Department must be a clear-headed lawyer. He must be familiar with the leading principles of jurisprudence as well as the practical details of judicial administration. To fulfil this qualification, he must, of course, be an English scholar. He must be conversant with those principles of International Law which have a bearing on our relations with our neighbours. It has to be remembered that it is this officer who has mainly to advise the Dewan in all judicial matters generally in disposing of appeals from the Varisht Court, in settling legal doubts or difficulties coming from all departments, in making laws and rules, and in conducting that portion of the correspondence with the Residency which relates to the extradition of criminals and to other matters involving judicial principles.

A properly qualified Head guarantees good government.

(6) If the Maharaja fails to secure a proper Head for the department under advertence, many difficulties and embarrassments are sure to be the consequence. Many things would, more or less, slide back into their old condition. Under the old re-

gime, extradition was involved in the greatest imaginable confusion. Extradition was exacted from Baroda by all around, but it was very imperfectly reciprocated to Baroda. The consequence was that our territories were the scene of numerous offences, the perpetrators of which could not be brough to punishment at all. Violent crimes were of every day occurrence. Life, person, and property were very insecure everywhere. Again, there was little that deserved the name of police, the consequenees of which might be better imagined than described. Again, there were no courts of justice deserving the name, the consequence of which also might be better imagined than described. In short, the Sirkar failed to fulfil the most elementary duties of a civilized government. Bearing all this in view, it will be seen that if the Maharaja has a proper head for the department under advertence, as is the case at present, it will be a great guarantee for good government.

The impression that no special qualifications are necessary for the post of the Head of the Military Department is not correct.

(7) Military, Settlement and Giras matters may well go, as they at present do under one department. The efficiency and good reputation of the administration largely depend upon the careful choice of the officer to be at the head of this department also. It is a department which deals with many matters of importance, of complexity, of difficulty, and of

delicacy. It also deals with many persons of consequence, or of a troublesome or turbulent character. The wisdom and experience and the judgment and tact of its present head have been of great service during these six years. Many practically useful principles and methods of transacting business and of settling disputes have now been attained in this department which deserve to be adhered to as the results of anxious reflection and laborious progress. The Maharaja has to be all the more careful in having a fully qualified officer at the head of the department under advertence, because an impression prevails among certain classes in the city that no special qualifications whatever are required for the post, that even the most ordinary person would be able to get through its duties. That impression arises from a misconception. The post of Civil Minister is mistaken for that of Commander-in-Chief of the Irregular Forces.

Grave abuses under the former regime.

(8) Under the former regime there was a lamentable want of system in the management of affairs connected with the Military, Settlement and Giras branches of business. It was, indeed, much worse than a want of system, for grave and manifold abuses prevailed. These have been mentioned in the Administration Reports, which, I hope, His Highness will go through. Many of these have been corrected and others are in course of

correction. The tendency of these abuses is to spring up again and again, and such tendency should be checked with firmness and vigilance and the process of correction should be steadly continued. For this purpose the head of the department should be, as already stated, a well qualified officer.

The Head of the Public Works Department.

(9) The Public Works Department is also one of the most important departments of the Huzur Cutcherry, and as such requires a duly qualified officer at its head. This officer, too, must be conversant with the English language, as he has to correspond with the Chief Engineer in English and to study English books bearing on Public Works. The present Head fulfils the requirements completely.

Duties of the several departmental Heads.

(10) The principal departments of the Huzur Cutcherry, I have above noticed, stand as follows :—

(1) Revenue Department.

(2) Military, Settlement, and Giras Departments.

(3) Judicial, Police, and Extradition Departments.

(4) Publc Works Department.

All these departments require for their heads first-rate officers, who will not only do their respective duties in a scientific, systematic, and satisfactory manner, but will, in conjunction with the Dewan, form the cabinet of the Maharaja—that is to say, that body of His Highness' ministers who will, under His Highness, be collectively responsible for the good government of the country.

(11) The primary responsibility for the good government of the country rests, of course, with the Maharaja himself. It is a weighty responsibility. It is a responsibility increasing with the general progress of India. It is a responsibility which must cause serious anxiety to the best of rulers. The only way in which His Highness can fulfil that heavy responsibility, is to have the best ministers for the conduct of the administration. These ministers should possess abundant intelligence, knowledge, experience and high character to command respect and to withstand hostile criticism from whatever quarter the same may come, either from British Authorities or from the general public. The very best Maharaja, with incompetent ministers, is pretty sure to be a failure.

Have the best ministers for the conduct of the administration.

(12) The demand for the best ministers is especially imperative in Baroda, because of its situation and circumstances. There is probably no other Native State in all India which has to deal with interests more involved, more intricate and more trying to the intellect. And there is probably no other Native State which is more exposed to public observation and criticism.

Demand for the best ministers imperative in Baroda.

(13) I have mentioned above four principal departments of the Huzur Cutcherry. These, however, do not comprise all the branches of business done there. There are numerous other branches besides, such as Accounts and Audits, Khangi, Education, Medicine, Municipalities, Boundary Settlement, General or Miscellaneous and last, not least, the English correspondence. On these I beg to offer a few observations.

A few observations on the other departments.

(*a*) Accounts and Audits are absolutely necessary for the proper conduct of the administration. They are necessary even in a private family, and they are much more necessary in a State. They should be entrusted as they at present are, to a distinct and specially qualified head. He must be versed in the old system of accounts and audit and also in the more improved modern system. He will largely assist the administration in keeping the finances in order.

(*a*) Accounts to be entrusted to a qualified head.

(*b*) The Khangi work may be given to some one of the heads of the principal departments. That work requires much watchfulness, judgment and tact. Extravagant and wasteful expenditure has to be kept within the limits fixed by His Highness. And yet, needless offence and annoyance have to be carefully avoided in the performance of this important and necessary duty.

(*b*) The Khangi to be entrusted to one of the heads.

(c) Education and Medicine.

(c) " Education " may also be given to some one of the heads of the principal departments. That head may be chosen for the purpose who is most familiar with the modern system of education. " Medicine " may go with education very well.

(d) Other minor branches.

(d) " Municipalities " may go with Public Works " Boundary Settlement " had better generally go under the Revenue Department. " General or Miscellaneous " may be with some one of the heads of the principal departments.

A fifth minister may be required.

(14) In process of time, as work increases, as it is sure to do, it may become desirable to put some of these branches of business under an additional or fifth minister. Indeed, I think that four ministers, as above stated would hardly suffice for the work of the administration, inasmuch as one of them might go away on leave, or might fall sick at any time.

Necessity of having a qualified Secretary in the English Correspondence Department.

(15) The English Correspondence Department of the Huzur Cutcherry is one of the most important departments. The credit of the whole administration largely depends upon the efficiency of this department. It is to be remembered that the Dewan has to carry on extensive correspondence in English and the correspondence with the Residency includes matters of great moment, dif-

ficulty, delicacy, or confidence. It is to be further remembered that the annual administration report is prepared and compiled in the English office of the Huzur Cutcherry. It is, therefore, essential that at the head of this office there should always be a thoroughly qualified Secretary or Manager like the present incumbent. He should be quite trustworthy, intelligent, well versed in English, able to write with ease and facility, active, energetic and industrious, possessing a good memory, and of a conciliatory disposition in order that he may communicate with the heads of the various other departments without friction.

The Fadnis and his duties.

(16) It remains that I shall say a few words about the Fadnis Department of the Huzur Cutcherry. The Fadnis is the Head of this Department. The Fadnis is a hereditary officer of the State, and it is desirable that it should be so. It is desirable to have a permanent element amidst so many shifting elements in the Huzur Cutcherry.

(*a*) Custodian of documents.

(*a*) The Fadnis is already the depository of the most valuable records of the past. He should continue to be so, and in this respect his usefulness should be extended. In fact, he should be the custodian of all valuable documents and decisions and of all important records of all departments. He will thus be a most useful referee.

(b) Another important function assigned to the Fadnis is to examine the cash balances in the Central Treasury and certify to their correctness. This should, by all means, be continued.

(b) Examining cash balances.

(c) Another important duty which the Fadnis has been doing is to write all or most of the orders to the Central Treasury involving money payments. In other words, he is the main channel of communication between the Huzur Cutcherry and the Central Treasury. This very judicious arrangement should also be continued.

(c) Writing all the orders to the Treasury involving payments.

(d) He also prepares all routine communications to be addressed to the Residency in the Vernacular. This may well be continued also.

(d) Preparing communications to the Residency.

(17) I may here suggest the desirableness of giving some assistance to the Fadnis in all these respects by placing under him two or three Darakdars, such as are doing no work, but are drawing considerable allowances.

The Fadnis may have two Darakdars under him.

CHAPTER XXXVIII

SALARIES

31*st August*, 1881.

Observations on the subject of salaries.

In connection with the Huzur Cutcherry and as applicable to all public establishments in general, I may here submit some observations on the subject of salaries. This is an important subject, regarding which His Highness should have clear ideas.

The idea that any man could fill any post.

(2) Formerly, almost any person, it was thought could fill any post and perform any duty. In such circumstances, there was no difficulty in getting persons for the public service. Shoals of candidates offered themselves when any vacancy occurred, and they would accept any salary, however low.

Why men could be got on low pay.

(3) Again, public servants in those days made plenty of money over and above their salaries. These were acquisitions which we, in these days, very properly deem unlawful and most discreditable. In short, and to speak plainly, they took bribes. They took employment not so much for the salary given as for the opportunity to plunder. There may have been exceptions, but I am speaking of the general

state of things. This is another reason why men could be got on low pay.

(4) The state of things now-a-days is very different. Happily the requirements of good administration are far better understood and appreciated. For the public service we now want educated men—men possessing the requisite qualifications—and men thoroughly upright and honorable who would not stoop to any unlawful gain. If we want a specially good article—not any article—we have to pay much higher for it. In other words, the State has to pay higher salaries.

The state must pay higher salaries.

(5) In regulating our salaries, we have to attend also to other considerations. There is a large demand in British India for educated and upright men. The remuneration which we offer to such men cannot be less than what the British Government offers. The Imperial service absorbs a great number of such men.

The salary not to be less than what the British offer.

(6) Again, in the British service, there is provision made for a retiring pension. As this is wanting here, the actual salary has to be made proportionately higher.

A retiring pension.

(7) Again, in the British service, the tenure of office is far more secure. The higher publc servants hold office during good behaviour. In other words,

The tenure of office to be more secure.

they are not liable to be turned out arbitrarily. On the other hand, in Native States generally, the case has, I am sorry to say, been considerably different. The best behaved public servant is not sure of retaining his appointment for any length of time. Indeed, it has not unfrequently occurred that the best behaved servants have been the least liked by the Maharaja, because their good principles would not allow them to do any dirty work which might be assigned to them. In consequence of this uncertainty as to tenure of office, good men look for much higher salary in the service of the Native State than in the British service. The higher salary has to cover the greater risk of losing the appointment itself.

The remarks about Native States in general not applicable to Baroda.

(8) Earnestly do I hope that what I have just said about Native States in general will not apply to Baroda under the rule of the carefully educated Prince who is about to assume power. Yet, obviously, public confidence cannot be gained in a day. It will take years of good government before public confidence becomes fairly established. Meanwhile the difference between the British service and that of the Native States in respect of security of tenure of office must be operating in reducing good men to demand higher pay in the latter than in the former service.

(9) Again, the earnings of educated and able men in the independent professions have much increased. A successful doctor or a successful pleader or merchant earns quite as much as he would have earned, had he entered the public service. The public service, too, has its influence in rendering it necessary to offer higher salaries in the service of the State.

The earnings of educated men have increased.

(10) Again, some of the Native States themselves are improving and therefore are adding to the demand for educated and upright men. The price of such men has increased on this account. No doubt, the supply of such men has also increased owing to the many educational agencies at work in different parts of India. Yet, the balance of effect is in favour of giving increased salaries to such men.

There is a demand for educated men.

(11) Considering the reasons above stated, it will be found that the scale of salaries adopted by the present administration is not excessive. This will be all the more evident, when it is noted that the heads of departments in the Huzur Cutcherry here are doing work really more difficult and responsible than that done by officers in the British service drawing equal pay. The matter may be regarded from another point of view. The existing salaries are not in truth so much higher than those of the

The present scale not excessive.

past as may seem to a cursory observer. The former salaries were, it should be recollected, largely supplemented by means of extra allowances in diverse shapes and from diverse sources. For instance, there were granted *chatri*, *masal*, *jabb*, *palki*, horses, *paga*, *warshassans*, *assamies* and villages. Moreover, there were shares in *nazrannas* sometimes. As to unrecognized or secret gains, these made a considerable addition. If all these things be included in the calculation, my belief is that the present rates are really lower, at any rate not higher.

Sirdars need not envy the salaries of officers.

(12) The Sirdars and Darakadars need not envy the existing salaries of the State officers because some of those Sirdars and Darakdars are themselves getting very large emoluments without any work to speak of.

Liberal salaries cut off corrupt acquisitions.

(13) It is undoubtedly some economy on the part of the State to give good, even liberal salaries to the higher functionaries of the State and thereby cut off corrupt acquisitions. It should be borne in mind that formerly for every corrupt acquisition of one thousand rupees made by an officer, he put the State probably to a loss of three or four or more thousand rupees. What the State may now be paying by way of salaries in excess of the past is, it must be remembered, manifold by the cessation of corruption.

(14) What I have just mentioned is only the pecuniary advantage accruing from good and liberal salaries. But the political advantages of having a set of able and upright men to conduct the administration are beyond estimate. Without such men, the administration would become despicable. The State would lead a sickly and weakly life which could not last very long. These various considerations forcibly point to the justice and expediency of maintaining the existing scale of salaries undiminished. In the lower grades of the service, some salaries will probably have to be yet increased.

The political advantages.

(15) I proceed now to another subject, which this seems to be an appropriate place to notice in. We have in the Huzur Cutcherry and other establishments several officers whose services have been borrowed from the British Government. A question here arises, " Is this right and proper, and is the State to continue to obtain the loan of British Government servants ? " On this topic, I beg to offer some remarks. The State has been most fortunate in having been able to obtain the services of the British Government servants we at present have in our establishments. On the deposition of Mulhar Rao, the work of reform which had to be done was one of great magnitude and seriousness, and its successful prosecution necessitated the assistance

The propriety of obtaining the loan of British Government servants.

of some trained and experienced hands. As these were not available at Baroda, they had to be got from outside, whether from the British Government service or elsewhere. They have done excellent service and have become even more valuable than ever before, because of the additional knowledge and experience they have gained in Baroda territories.

They diffuse their knowledge.

(16) These officers should, of course, continue to serve the State not only because their services are in themselves so valuable but also because they are instrumental in diffusing their own knowledge and experience around them.

The necessity of engaging them may ultimately disappear.

(17) As our own people learn business and get trained, the necessity for borrowing outsiders may be expected to diminish and to ultimately disappear. This is a result much to be desired. It must be steadily kept in prospect and pressed forward, too, in earnest.

Advantages and disadvantages attaching to Native British servants lent to the State.

(18) It is here desirable to take a view of the advantages and disadvantages attaching to Native British servants taken on loan by the State.

(a) Higher salaries.

(*a*) In the first place the State has to pay them much higher salaries than they draw in the British service, to induce them to come and work in our service. We have to pay at least 50 per cent. more, not frequently even 100 per cent, more.

(b) Pension contribution.

(b) Then we have to pay their pension contribution to the British Government, and this is a further additional charge.

(c) Possibility of leaving service.

(c) Then there is the possibility of their leaving our service at any time and reverting to that of the British Government.

(d) Misbehaviour.

(d) Again, if any of them misbehaves and has to be dismissed, the State has to take care that the dismissal is upon such strong grounds as to satisfy the British Government also of their validity.

(e) They are too technical.

(e) They are, generally speaking, a little too regular and technical, at least at the beginning of their service in the Native States. I mean that they are guided more by rules than by principles. In other words, they are somewhat defective in that elasticity which the circumstances of the Native States require.

(f) They lack the qualities of statesmanship.

(f) Also, generally speaking, they are imperfect in the qualities of statesmanship for the simple reason that, in the British service, they fill very subordinate posts—that they do not rise to those higher positions which necessitate the acquisition and exercise of those qualities. In the vast and complex machine of the Imperial Government they turn some distance with almost mechanical regularity without learning—without having to learn—all about the machine as a whole and as composed of parts all dependent on one another, and each contributing its share to the fulfilment of the common purpose.

(*g*) A large field of selection.

(*g*) On the other hand, the facilities afforded by the British Government for our obtaining the loan of their servants, enable the Native State to have the advantage of a very large field of selection—to choose from so large a field men of tried and trained ability and probity—to pick out men just suited to given requirements.

(*h*) A public servant independent of local connections.

(*h*) It is also a great advantage that the Native State is thus enabled to occasionally introduce into its service a public servant independent of local connections, of local combinations and of local prejudices.

(*i*) Increase of efficiency.

(*i*) Another considerable advantage of such introduction is that the British servant, thoroughly trained as he is in his particular work, is instrumental in having many under him in the Native service and thereby raising the standard of efficiency. And I will only add that a carefully selected British servant introduced into the service of the Native State, becomes very valuable after some years' experience in Native administration. Of this, there are bright examples at this moment in our Huzur Cutcherry.

One or two warnings.

(19) It is not out of place here to suggest one or two warnings. The high character of the administration being a matter of vital importance, the Native State should scrupulously avoid introducing into its service any persons who have been dismissed from the service of the British Government for gross misconduct importing moral depravity. Such persons, will offer themselves for employment on cheap terms. They will press themselves on the Maharaja's attention in various ways. But they must be firmly rejected ; they would say that they do not want any salary, but they simply desire to be in attendance upon His Highness and to make themselves useful in miscellaneous ways, as for instance, in giving private information, in discussing matters and offering counsels in writing to the newspapers, etc., etc. But my opinion is that the Maharaja should summarily reject all such overtures.

The practice of engaging British retired servants indiscriminately is not desirable.

(20) Nor should the Native State indiscriminately take into its service such British servants as have retired on pension. As a general rule, those who have been deemed unfit to render further service under the British Government,

must be equally unfit to render further service under the Native Government. Instances, however, sometimes occur in which a pensioned British servant still retains the capacity to work. There is no objection to employ such person for a time in the service of the Native State, if he possesses more than ordinary merit.

Salary to be one lump sum.

(21) Formerly, the remuneration of our public servants was a conglomerate of salaries, *assamies*, *warshassans*, lands, fees, *palki* allowances, etc., etc. It was altogether a most confused and complex matter. It was a system of concealment, deception and fraud. It made it difficult for the Maharaja to know what the total remuneration of any servant was. And it often happened—it happened too frequently that though the service was dispensed with, some and even several items of the remuneration continued to be paid! This has now been happily done away with, and every care has to be taken against its resuscitation. A public servant should have a defined salary in the lump and in cash, and this should cease the moment the man ceases to be a public servant.

CHAPTER XXXIX

PUBLIC SERVICE.

14th September, 1881.

An extensive organisation.

The public service constitutes an extensive organisation which is felt in every part of the country and which comes in contact with the people in all their relations with the government of the country. Every part of this organisation should be made sound and further means should be devised to provide for the continuity of the soundness.

Heads of departments to have powers.

(2) The heads of the various departments being proper men, they should have powers liberally given them for making appointments, promotions, etc. They should have powers also to fine, suspend, dismiss, etc. Without such powers, they would not be able to maintain discipline and efficiency. The very essence of an efficient organization is that subordinates should be grouped together under superior officers and that the latter should have the means of influencing the hopes of the former.

Right principles to guide them in the exercise of their power.

(3) The heads of departments should exercise their powers above-mentioned not arbitrarily or just as they like but under the guidance of right principles. What these principles are may be observed from a circular order sent in A. D. 1875 by the existing administration.

The Ruler to supervise and control.

(4) His Highness the Maharaja, in the exercise of supervision and control, has to see that the provisions of the circular order are generally attended to. The result will be that the public service will be required, from time to time, so as not only to maintain but to improve its efficiency.

The opinion of the head in matters of patronage to carry much weight.

(5) It is the head of the Department who can most correctly know what qualifications are required for any given post under him and whether a given candidate possesses these qualifications. He best knows also which of his subordinates has earned promotion, etc. Therefore, as a rule, his opinion in matters of patronage should carry much weight.

Advice of selfish persons.

(6) Ignorant or selfish persons will advise the Maharaja to concentrate all the patronage in his own hands and to make appointments without reference and even contrary to the views of the heads of departments. The sagacity of His Highness will sum-

marily reject such advice as prejudicial to organisation and efficiency.

Promote efficiency.

(7) The primary object being to appoint and promote the most efficient persons, recommendations conflicting with that object should be rejected, from whatever quarter they may come. For instance, such recommendations may come from friends and relations. They may come from British Officers, they may come from the newspapers. The Maharaja's firmness may be abundantly exercised in steadily pursuing the primary object aforesaid.

Favours to be sparingly shown.

(8) Cases may sometimes occur, in which His Highness wishes to show favour to a particular person irrespective of his merits and qualifications. Such cases of course, must be few and far between. Better, then, to appoint such person to some quiet sinecure post in which he would do no harm than to place him in charge of duties which he could not perform satisfactorily.

Transfers not to be made indiscriminately.

(9) Another point to be kept in view by His Highness is this. The public service has various branches. Each branch requires its own special qualifications. It follows that a person who answers well in one branch would not necessarily answer well in another branch. Therefore, transfers from one

branch to another should not be made indiscriminately. The caution herein given applies particularly to the Revenue and Judicial Departments of the State.

Nazaranas and bribes for appointments are a poison to Government.

(10) The Maharaja should never take any *nazaranna* for any appointment or promotion in the public service. His Highness should not allow any one to receive any bribe for any appointment or promotion. It is a poison which is fatal to all good government and must be shunned as such. Whoever acts contrary to this principle should be expelled from the service whether private or public, and should be liable to an unsparing criminal prosecution.

How unscrupulous men may tempt a ruler.

(11) There is another way in which bad and unscrupulous men tempt a Maharaja to appoint them to considerable and responsible posts. For instance, one of them says to His Highness, "Give me such an appointment, and I will increase the revenue by such an amount." The money-loving Maharaja swallows the bait. And what is the consequence ? Simply the misery of the subject population. That certainly is not the way to increase revenue. That increase of revenue alone is creditable which results from steady good government, from the increased wealth and prosperity of the people and not from increased exactions.

Bad Government due to an ignorant exercise of the rights of patronage.

(12) The several suggestions I have offered in this paper deserve attentive consideration on the part of the Maharaja; indeed, they need to be carefully studied, because I know from actual experience that many evils and troubles arise in Native States from want of a clear comprehension of principles on which patronage should be exercised. Much of the bad governemnt of Native States, and much of the dangers to which Native Princes become exposed, is due to an ignorant exercise of the rights of patronage.

CHAPTER XL

RELATIONS WITH BRITISH GOVERNMENT.

Wednesday, 21st September, 1881

Relations with the British Government to be carefully studied.

Nothing is more important than that the Maharaja should study carefully and thoroughly the relations of his State with the British Government. They involve many momentous, difficult and delicate matters, of which the Maharaja should have an accurate and complete knowledge. Upon such knowledge depends in a very large measure His Highness's safety, honour, strength and happiness. I have no doubt, therefore, that the observations I am going to offer will receive the utmost attention.

The British Government exercises supreme sway.

(2) There are some broad facts which must, at the outset, be fully and clearly realized, and I proceed to state them. The first and foremost fact is, that the British Government exercises supreme sway over India from Cape Comorin to the Himalayas and from Calcutta to Peshawar. The area of this imperial sway comprises both the British territories

and the territories ruled by the Native Princes. It is the British Government which maintains the general peace of this vast tract.

Their power is a combination of physical with intellectual and moral power.

(3) The British Government fulfils this great function with a power which is irresistible. It is a power which could crush resistance singly or combined and from whatever quarter in India it might arise. This power of the British Government is all the more irresistible because it is derived from a combination of physical with intellectual and moral power. Owing to this happy combination the British Empire in India is far more powerful and far more durable than any empire which had preceded the same.

Every Native Ruler to conciliate the British Government.

(4) It follows that every Native Prince should conciliate the British Government which possesses such irresistible power. It would be the greatest folly for any Native Prince to provoke it seriously against him. This must be unmistakably understood. Conciliation is an absolute and unavoidable necessity of the situation and circumstances. This necessity must be accepted, and if accepted cheerfully, so much the better in the interests of the Native Princes.

Conciliation not difficult.

(5) Happily, however, the character and qualities of the British Government are such that conciliation is not difficult or costly.

(6) Moreover, while the British Government is physically irresistible, it wisely permits itself beyond all example to be irresistible in the peaceful field of reason, justice and morality. It is anxious to abstain from everything unreasonable, unjust or immoral. The consequence of this anxiety is that, if it ever be unconsciously led into any unreasonable, unjust or immoral action, you have only to prove to it that the action is such and it may generally be expected to withdraw from such action. This is a great and distinguishing characteristic of the British Government. It is this noble quality of the British Government which greatly restrains the abuse of its irresistible physical power. It is this quality which protects the Native States from becoming the victims of the lawless exercise of that power. It is this quality from which the Native States derive the hope of living securely, honourably, happily and long.

The noble quality of the British Government.

Conclusions on which the native Ruler should build his policy.

(7) The conclusions we have reached may be thus very briefly stated, namely :—

(*a*) The Native Prince should recognize the power of the British Government as irresistible.

(*b*) He may depend upon it that the British Government, though possessing resistible power, is amenable to reason;

justice, etc., and morality, and is therefore open to argument.

(*c*) The British Government may be conciliated without much difficulty or cost.

Upon these simple axioms should the Native Prince build his whole policy.

Never think of coercing the British by physical force.

(8) I will now briefly state what his whole policy should accordingly be. He should never think of coercing the British Government by means of physical force. The British Government should have no reason given it to suspect any such thought on the part of the Native Prince. He should avoid the maintenance or increase of needless troops. He should not store up needless arms and ammunition. He should not set up the secret manufactories of military stores. He should not show the remotest disposition to combine with those who may be hostile or even unfriendly to the British Government whether they be individuals or nations. He should not join or support any political agitation directed against, or embarrassing to the British Government. These broad hints suffice for the purpose in view and may be suggestive of any minor hints in the same direction.

Appreciate the benefits of British rule.

(9) Further, the Native Prince should show a cordial appreciation of the great benefits which India in general, and

the Native States in particular, undoubtedly enjoy under British supremacy.

Argue on grounds of reason, justice and morality.

(10) The Native Prince may, when any differences arise with the British Government, respectfully argue with that Government, on the grounds of reason, justice and morality. It is in this peaceful manner and in this manner only, that the Native Prince can defend his rights, honour and privileges and interests of his subjects. He must appeal to those principles of reason, justice and morality by which the British Government has repeatedly declared itself bound.

Govern your state well.

(11) He should conciliate the British Government, which, as already stated, it is not difficult or costly to do. The best means of conciliating the British Government in these days is for the Native Prince to govern his own State well, and also to see that his arrangements are not in such conflict with those of the British Government as to be a source of constant irritation or annoyance to the British Government. Any Native Prince, who steadily pursues the policy thus indicated, is sure to get on smoothly and well. His security, his happiness and his durability are insured so long as the British Government endures in India and is true to its own declared principles. This will be very long. Indeed, human foresight cannot assign any limit of time in this respect.

Contrast the present with the past.

(12) Just mark here, please, the contrast—the very great contrast which this state of things presents to that which existed before the establishment of British supremacy in India. In the Moghlai and even in the Maratha period, no Native Prince enjoyed any sense of security. Uncertainty, strife, confusion and anarchy prevailed in their most intensified forms. Just note how the Gaekwar suffered even at the hands of the Maratha Government at Poona. The sufferings of the people in general were even greater than those of the Prince. History bears abundant evidence.

What these principles of reason, justice and morality are:—

(13) As I have already said, the Native Prince may when any differences arise with the British Government, respectfully argue with that Government on the grounds of reason, justice, and morality. In defence of his rights, honour and privileges and the interests of his subjects, he may respectfully appeal to those principles of reason, justice and morality, by which the British Government has repeatedly declared itself bound. It becomes, therefore, very important that the Maharàja and his Ministers should be acquainted with the chief of those principles. Let us go over some of these, drawing them from such sources as are at this moment within our reach.

(a) I must begin by referring to that great document—Her Majesty's Proclamation of A. D. 1858. One paragraph of it runs thus: "We desire no extension of our present territorial possessions, and while we will permit no aggression upon our dominions or our rights to be attempted with impunity, we shall sanction no encroachment on those of others." One great principle which we derive from the above is that the British Government has solemnly bound itself not to take any territory from any Native State. Upon no grounds or pretexts whatever will the British Government take any territory from any Native State. The British Government will thus resist one great temptation; the Native States are thus freed from one great danger. The whole constitutes a solemn and permanent guarantee for the continued existence of the Native States in their territorial integrity. The Native States must be profoundly grateful for this great security.

(a) The proclamation of 1858. The British Government will not take territory from any Native State.

(b) The foregoing assurance, however, does not mean that the British Government will never deprive a Native Prince of his territories—that it will never depose a Native Prince. The British Government does retain this power. If a Native Prince is guilty of gross misgovernment, the British Government has the power to depose him. Simi-

(b) Though a Ruler may be deposed, the state will be preserved.

larly if a Native Prince is grossly disloyal to the British Government and becomes its enemy or joins its enemies, the British Government may depose such a Prince. But even in that case the British Government will not annex to itself the territories of the deposed Prince. Though the Prince may be deposed, the Native State will be preserved in its integrity. Some other person—probably some heir or relative of the deposed Prince—will be put in possession of the Native State. Though the ruler may be changed for some sufficient reason, the Native State itself will remain in its territorial integrity.

Example of the above.

The principle was fully exemplified in the instance of Baroda itself. Mulhar Rao Gaekwar was deposed and a distant relative of his was substituted. But Her Majesty's word was fully kept, inasmuch as not one inch of the Baroda territories was taken away by the British Government.

(c) Where lineal descendants fail.

(*c*) Even where lineal descendants fail in the case of a Native Prince, the British Government will not take the Raj, but will give it to the nearest or one of the nearest of the surviving relatives.

(d) Adoption of sons by native Princes.

(*d*) The British Government also recognizes the adoption of sons by the Native Princes, which is a course equally of justice and good policy. It may be stated here merely for information that the right of Native Princes to adopt heirs has been recognized by the British Government mainly from the period Her Majesty the Queen assumed the direct government of India.

(e) Exchange of territory by mutual consent.

(*e*) The part of the Queen's Proclamation under remark does not, however, prevent exchanges of territory by mutual consent.

(f) Aggression on the British dominions not allowed.

(*f*) Her Majesty will punish any aggression on her dominions or on her right. Nothing need be said on this point, because Baroda has never attempted any such aggression and never will attempt the same.

(g) No encroachments on the rights of others.

(*g*) Her Majesty will sanction no encroachment on the dominions or rights of others. This refers principally to the Native Princes and secures their protection.

The continuance of the Native States is the desire of the British.

(14) All these things being considered, the British Government has bound itself to protect the Native States to an extent and in a manner unknown to the preceding History of India. This is undoubtedly a matter of the highest satisfaction to all India, because all India most earnestly desires the continuance of the Native States.

CHAPTER XLI

Relations with British Government

Wednesday 28th September, 1881.

Social advancement can be secured by peace and good Government.

Another very important paragraph of Her Majesty's Proclamation is now to be noticed. It runs as follows :—

" We shall respect the rights, dignity and honor of Native Princes as our own. And we desire that they as well as our own subjects should enjoy that prosperity and that social advancement which can only be secured by internal peace and good government." These are just, generous and noble assurances proceeding from the highest authority of the British Government. They are assurances which greatly fortify the Native Princes and their States.

The rights and honour of Native Princes to be respected.

(2) Let us note that the rights, dignity and honour of Native Princes are not only to be respected, but are to be respected as if they were Her Majesty's own. The assurance is thus as full and complete as the most ardent well-wisher of Native States could wish. It is a strong and solemn assurance which is the outcome of that exalted moral principle or precept of religion, whether Hindu or Christian,

which bids us treat others as we would they should treat us. The rights, dignity and honour or Native Princes are thus secured in the strongest manner possible.

The rights claimed should be reasonable.

(3) In connection with this, however, one thing should be carefully remembered. The Native Princes should not claim any rights, dignity and honour, which are extravagant or unusual or incompatible with civilized society and civilized Government. What they may claim and what Her Majesty has graciously and solemnly promised to respect, are reasonable rights, dignity and honour.

Examples of rights not reasonably exercised.

(4) For instance, it would not be reasonable for any Native Prince to claim the right of forcibly taking into his zenana any woman he likes. It would not be reasonable for him to claim the right of arbitrarily putting any person into prison. It would not be reasonable for him to claim the right of making the British Resident sit on the floor without a chair, while he (the Prince) himself sits high on the *Gadee.* It would not be reasonable for him to claim any rights which are contrary to the treaties and engagements by which he is bound. The few examples just given will serve to show what is meant and what is not meant by the paragraph of the Queen's Proclamation under advertence. The warning which they suggest may not

be quite unnecessary because it is not impossible that a Prince, in a moment of haste, might presume too much on this part of the Proclamation and get into serious trouble.

The British Government is superior to that of the Native Princes.

(5) From the words, "We shall respect the rights, etc., of Native Princes as our own," it will not be inferred that Her Majesty places the Princes on a footing of equality with herself. From the very nature of things equality does not and cannot exist. The British Government is decidedly superior to the Native Princes in many essential respects, and especially in respect to power and influence. This is a fact which daily stares us in the face and no Native Prince can ignore it. What the words of the Queen's Proclamation mean is, that the rights, dignity and honour of Native Princes whatever they are, and as they are, will be respected and will be respected as much as if they were Her Majesty's own.

The rulers to promote internal peace and Government.

(6) In the paragraph of the Proclamation under notice, Her Majesty declares the important truth that prosperity and social advancement can be secured only by internal peace and good government. In desiring, therefore, that the Native Princes should enjoy prosperity and social advancement, Her Majesty clearly desires that these Princes should promote internal peace

and government. It is, of course, the duty of every Prince to promote peace and good government; and the aforesaid declaration of Her Majesty makes this duty all the more imperative.

The British Government will maintain all treaties with the Native Princes.

(7) Another paragraph of the Queen's Proclamation declares that all treaties and engagements made with the Native Princes will be scrupulously maintained, and further declares that Her Majesty looks for a like observance on the part of the Princes. Though possessing irresistible power, the British Government thus distinctly declares that it is bound by the treaties and engagements with the Native Princes. In other words, the British Government will scrupulously do all that the treaties and engagements promise and scrupulously abstain from doing all that they forbid. The declaration is the very foundation of the continued existence and security of the Native Prince.

Who in return should do the same thing.

(8) On the other hand, the Native Princes are expected to observe the treaties and engagements in the most scrupulous manner. This is obviously most right and proper. The Princes should therefore make themselves thoroughly, minutely and accurately acquainted with the treaties and engagements, carefully note everything which requires to be done or requires not to be done and

38

scrupulously act accordingly. The Princes should be more careful not to give reason, or even the appearance of reason, to the British Government to say, "You have not observed the treaties and engagements, you cannot therefore expect us to observe them."

Peaceful industry and works of public utility to be promoted.

(9) The Queen's Proclamation concludes with the expression of a noble resolve which deserves to be taken to heart by every ruler, small or great. That resolve is expressed in the following memorable words :—"It is our earnest desire to stimulate the peaceful industry of India, to promote works of public utility and improvement and to administer its Government for the benefit of all our subjects resident therein. In their prosperity will be our strength, in their contentment our security, and in their gratitude our best reward."

Govern for the benefit of all.

(10) The more then, the Native Princes follow this noble example of a Sovereign much greater than any one of them and much greater even then all of them put together, the more will they be in accord with, and the more will they be esteemed by, the Imperial Government which, as already stated, holds sway over all India, with irresistible power, and which effectually protects each of them against another's aggression and protects all against foreign

aggression. Each Native Prince should similarly resolve to govern for the benefit of all his subjects and not for the selfish pleasure and enjoyment of himself, and a narrow circle of friends and dependents. Let each Native Prince proudly say that in the prosperity of his subjects will be his strength, in their contentment his security, and in their gratitude his best reward.

Importance of those principles.

(11) We have thus derived some large and invaluable principles from Her Majesty's Proclamation in its bearing on the Native States—principles which restrain and control the action of the irresistible power of the British Government, principles without which that irresistible power would be an unmitigated curse to India. Let us now proceed to notice other principles which regulate the relations between the British Government and the Native States.

The duty of the British Government to protect the Native State against the violence of another.

(12) It is to be remembered that the British Government has undertaken the duty of protecting each Native State against the aggression or violence of another. This duty gives the British Government the right to see that each Native State does not provoke the aggression or violence of another. It is thus that the British Government has the right to prevent a Native State's aggression or violence against

another Native State and also the right to prevent such action on the part of a Native State as would provoke the aggression or violence of another Native State. In this respect the British Government acts the part of a grand and powerful political magistrate over the Native States. Such a magistrate must necessarily have the right to restrain transgression by Native States.

Correspondence between two States.

(13) Hence it is that the British Government tells every Native State not to carry on direct correspondence with any other Native State. All correspondence between one Native State and another must pass through the offices of the British Government.

The Native State to refer disputes to the British Government

(14) Hence it is that the British Government tells every Native State to refer to British officers every dispute or difference between it and any other Native State. The British Government takes means to bring about a just and peaceful settlement which must be submitted to by the Native States concerned. The British Government has the right to enforce its settlements thus effected.

The Native State not to provoke aggression from foreign powers.

(15) Again, it should be remembered that the British Government has undertaken the duty of protecting each Native State against aggression or volence from foreign powers. Such

as Russia, France, Germany, the United States of America, etc., etc. This duty gives the British Government the right to see that each Native State carefully abstains from provoking aggression or violence from such foreign powers.

The rights of the British Government.

(16) It is thus that the British Government has the right to prevent such action on the part of a Native State as would provoke a foreign power. Hence it is that the British Government tells every Native State not to carry on direct correspondence with any foreign power. Hence it is that the British Government has the right to compel any Native State to make any immediate reparation for any injury it may have caused to any foreign power, as for instance, by unjustly imprisoning a subject of the foreign power, by unjustly depriving him of life or property, by plundering any foreign vessel wrecked on the coast of the Native State; and so forth.

The Native Prince not to provoke his subjects by misgovernment.

(17) Again, be it remembered that the British Government has undertaken, wherever treaties regarding a subsidiary force exist, to protect the Native Prince against the violence of his own subjects. This duty gives the British Government the right to see that the Native Prince does not provoke by gross misgovernment his own subjects to violence.

(18) This point is clearly put in the following words of a high officer of the British Government He says: "The objection to protect the Prince from the dangers of internal anarchy or insurrection, from whatever cause it may arise, appears to involve the corresponding privilege of interfering to arrest the progress of proceedings tending to produce it; and the necessity of such interference is the greater and more frequent, because all the States of India being (with some few partial exceptions) purely monarchical, the good government of the country must ever depend upon the personal character and qualifications of the Prince."

Good government depends on the personal character of the ruler.

(19) The same view was put forth very recently and very strongly in the case of Baroda itself. It was done by His Excellency the Viceroy (Lord Northbrook) in his *Khureeta* to His Highness Mulhar Rao Gaekwad, dated 25th July, 1874. The Viceroy emphatically said, "My friend, I cannot consent to employ British troops to protect any one in a course of wrong-doing. Misrule on the part of a Government which is upheld by the British power is misrule, in the responsibility for which the British Government becomes, in a measure, involved. It becomes, therefore, not only the right but the positive duty of the British Government to see that the administration of a State in such a condition is

Lord Northbrook on Misrule.

reformed, and that the gross abuses are removed."
* * * * * * "If these obligations be not fulfilled, if gross misgovernment be permitted, if substantial justice be not done to the subjects of the Baroda State, if life and property be not protected, or if the general welfare of the country and people be persistently neglected, the British Government, will assuredly intervene in the manner which, in its judgment, may be best calculated to remove these evils and to secure good government. Such timely intervention, indeed, to prevent misgovernment culminating in the ruin of the State is no less an act of friendship to the Gaekwar himself than a duty to his subjects."

The British will interfere to prevent misrule.

(20) It follows that when the British Government is bound to protect a Native Prince against the violence of his own subjects, that government has the right to intervene to prevent such gross misrule by the Prince as might provoke the violence of his own subjects.

The rights of interference with a Native State.

(21) Again, the British Government derives rights of interference with a Native State from the specific provisions (where such exist) of the existing treaties and engagements. The nature and extent of the interference under reference must be determined by the express terms of those documents. It may here be useful to take a brief and collective

view of the interference which the British Government may exercise with a Native State as shown above.

(*a*) It may interfere in the relations of the Native State with other Native States.

(*b*) It may interfere in the relations of the Native States with Foreign Powers.

(*c*) It may interfere in the internal administration of the Native State to prevent or correct such gross misrule as would provoke popular rising.

(*d*) It may interfere in the internal administration of the Native State, in the manner and to the extent specially provided in the treaties and engagements with the Native State.

It is useless to resist interference.

(22) All this should be clearly understood and remembered and recognised. It would not be desirable nor would it be of any use to resist or even to deprecate such interference on the part of the British Government.

CHAPTER XLII

INTERNAL ADMINISTRATION OF NATIVE STATES

12th, 19th and 26th October, 1881.

When the British Government may interfere.

The last time we met here, we concluded with a brief and collective view of the interference which the British Government may exercise with a Native State, namely, under the following heads:—

(*a*) In the relations of the Native State with other Native States.

(*b*) In the relations of the Native State with Foreign Powers.

(*c*) In the internal administration of the Native State to prevent or correct such gross misrule as might provoke popular rising requiring for its suppression the use of the British subsidiary force.

(*d*) In the internal administration of the Native State, in the manner and to the extent specially provided in the treaties and engagements with the Native State.

(2) We must recognise such interference in certain contingencies as necessary and unavoidable. I go further and say that such interference may be recognised as highly beneficial.

Such interference necessary.

(3) Of course, the British Government should not and would not exercise any such interference unless there was occasion calling for the same. It follows that if the Native State conducts its affairs with due care and wisdom, it may mostly, perhaps altogether avoid giving occasion for the interference of the British Government.

Let the Native State avoid giving occasion for interference.

(4) Such being the case, it becomes worth while to see more in detail how the Native State may avoid giving occasion for the active interference of the British Governmnt under each of the four heads aforesaid.

How the Native State may avoid giving occasion.

(*a*) The Native State should carefully attend to the following points in connection with the head (*a*)

(*a*) Relations with other Native States.

(i) Do not correspond directly with any Native State. All such correspondence should be addressed to the British Resident or through him. This is already an established practice which should be strictly adhered to. The spirit of the rule just stated requires abstention from allowing any ser-

(i) Correspondence how to be carried on.

vant or subordinate of one State or Chief to correspond with a servant or subordinate of another State or Chief in behalf of their respective States or Chiefs. Even oral messages should be abstained from.

(ii) Meeting any Chief personally.

(ii) Do not personally meet any Chief unless with the knowledge of the British Resident. Meeting any Chief with the knowledge of the British Resident, do not hold any conversation with that Chief such as may be disrespectful or offensive to the British Government.

(iii) Treat the Chief with honour.

(iii) Always treat the Chief with the courtesy and marks of honour due to him. He should have no reason to complain to British authorities in this respect.

(iv) Give the Chief his recognised titles.

(iv) In every communication which may have to be addressed regarding any Chief, or his important Officers, or their action, give them their full recognised titles, and use courteous language. Abstain from imputing to them any bad motives. Abstain from violently criticising their action. In short, abstain from everything offensive or disrespectful.

(v) Giving police assistance.

(v) Render hearty police assistance to every Native State in the detection and apprehension of its offenders and in the tracing out of its stolen property, and also in surrendering the offenders and the stolen property.

(vi)Treat all the subjects alike.

(vi) In matters of civil and criminal justice, and also in those of general trade, treat the subjects of every Native State quite like your own subjects. I mean that no unfavourabe distinction should be made in regard to them.

(vii)Avoid boundary disputes.

(vii) Avoid boundary disputes to the utmost extent possible by the necessary precautions. If, however, any occur, earnestly prevent breaches of the peace of every sort, and refer the dispute to the proper British authorities for their investigation and decision. When a boundary dispute has been demarcated by permanent pillars, see that these pillars are scrupulously preserved.

(viii) Render help to the Chief whenever necessary.

(viii) When a Chief happens to possess *wanta* or other private landed property in these territories, render him cordial assistance in the recovery of his rents, in the settlement of his disputes with his tenants, etc.

When a Chief happens to have *Giras* allowance from our Treasury, see that it is punctually paid to him.

In the construction of roads and bridges affecting the interests of both the territories, render due co-operation.

In short, respect in your turn, the rights, honour and dignity of every Chief as your own.

By steadily acting on these principles, we shall avoid giving occasion to the British Government to interfere with us under the head marked (*a*) above I may here state that these principles almost equally apply to the relations of this State with its neighbouring British districts and British officers.

(*b*) Relations with foreign powers.

(*b*) Proceeding to the next head marked (*b*), I invite attention to the following points in connection therewith.

(i) Avoid unpleasant collisions with Europeans.

(i) It is to be remembered that in consequence of the facilities afforded by steam communication, the subjects of various European and American States travel abroad very much and may be, more or less, and now and then, met with in the territories of this Native State—I mean the subjects of England, France, Germany, Austria, Italy, Russia, the American Union, etc., etc., etc. For the purpose of brevity, I will call all of them "Europeans," which I may do as they all belong to the European race. It is to be also remembered that whatever the European may be, the Government to which he belongs exercises a certain degree of protection over him. It will not allow him to be subjected to any gross violence or injustice anywhere, much less in a Native State. It follows that we must be very careful as regards any European in our territories. To state the matter briefly and generally we must, to the utmost extent possible, avoid unpleasant collisions with Europeans. This is the main key of the policy to be pursued. I will, however, state some details.

(ii) Let the European have a proper introduction.

(ii) If a European stranger appears here and seeks an interview with the Maharaja, His Highness should see him only if he has brought a proper introduction. He can always bring an introductory note from the British Resident. If the European stranger has brought no proper introduction, His Highness had better refer him to the Residency. If any European gentlemen comes here properly introduced, show him all due courtesy and consideration.

(iii) When they commit errors, give warning.

(iii) European strangers are prone to commit errors or give offence in Native States from ignorance of native habits and feelings. Be indulgent to them in this respect. For instance, a European may enter a native temple which he ought not to enter. He may shoot a peacock where such proceeding is highly offensive. He may be found fishing at some ghaut held sacred by the native community, and so forth. In such cases, no attempt should be made to punish him. Give him a gentle warning, and this will generally suffice, if not, move the British Resident.

(iv) Interdict searching their baggage.

(iv) Europeans have a great aversion to their baggage being searched for contraband or dutiable articles. They have a great aversion also to being detained by Custom's officers. Therefore, as much as possible, interdict such searches and detentions in ordinary cases. Where merchants and goods for trade are concerned, they must, of course, submit to the ordinary rules.

(v) Avoid contracts with them.

(v) As much as may be fairly possible, avoid entering into any contracts with Europeans for supplies in the service, execution of works, etc; and where some few contracts are unavoidably entered into, perform your part of them with the most scrupulous exactitude.

(vi) No pecuniary dealings with them.

(vi) Have little or no pecuniary dealings with Europeans, such as lending or borrowing. This, however, does not apply to our purchasing British Government securities or keeping a current account with such a bank as that of Bombay.

(vii) Their safety, while travelling.

(vii) Take precautions that European travellers are not robbed in these territories.

(viii) No European to suffer personal ill-treatment.

(viii) See that no European suffers any personal ill-treatment in these territories at the hands of the people. If, unfortunately, a European happens to have suffered such, promptly and fully punish the offenders. I avail myself of this opportunity to make known one important and well-recognised principle, namely, that when a European has suffered an injury at the hands of our people the like of which he might suffer in his own country and indeed, in any country however civilized, we become relieved of responsibility on that account, provided we trace out the authors of the injury and subject them to just punishment, and to reparation so far as may be possible in the circumstances of the case. By doing this, we shall have done as much as the sufferer's own Government would have done in similar circumstances, and no more could be reasonably expected of us. But if, on the other hand, we fail to trace out the offenders and subject them to just punishment and reparation and especially if this failure is due to imperfect arrangements for the security of life and property, or to negligence or indifference or anything worse in a particular case, then we shall be held, more or less and sometimes fully responsible for the injury caused by our people.

(ix) Offences by British European officers to be referred to the Resident.

(ix) In cases of minor offences by British European officers, such as beating or otherwise ill-treating our people, forcibly taking supplies from them, behaving disrespectfully to our authorities, etc., etc., represent the matter correctly and calmly to the

British, Resident, who will readily bring about a departmental disposal of the matter. The European officer concerned will probably be transferred, or degraded, or otherwise made to suffer for his misbehaviour.

(x) Giving redress.

(x) If any European seeks any kind of redress in these territories, whether criminal, civil, or political, promptly attend to his complaint and grant such redress as he may be justly entitled to.

(xi) Giving help to the Shipwrecked crew.

(xi) If any ship be wrecked on any of our coasts, render every possible assistance, in order to save the passengers, crew and cargo. Shipwrecks, however, will be very few, now that we are providing the requisite lighthouses.

(xii) No European to reside or settle.

(xii) Do not permit any European to reside or settle in these territories and do not employ him in the public or palace service, unless after duly consulting the British Resident and obtaining through that authority the sanction of the Government of India. I include in the public service a pleader in courts or cutcherries.

(xiii) European vagrants.

(xiii) European vagrants should be promptly sent out of these territories by moving the British Resident to take the necessary action.

(xiv) It is within the range of possibility that, in certain circumstances or contingencies, secret emissaries from European countries, hostilely or adversely disposed towards the British Government, may come here to incite disaffection towards that Government. Be very much on your guard against such emissaries. Do not fail to inform the British Resident of everything you come to know of them. The various suggestions I have thus made, though they may not be exhaustive, will probably suffice to indicate the character or spirit of the policy which the Maharaja should pursue in this respect.

(xiv) Emissaries from hostile European countries.

(*c*) We have now to notice the head marked (*c*) above. I will offer a few preliminary remarks and then offer a few detailed practical suggestions as to the policy to be pursued.

(c) Internal administration.

(i) It is the right of the Maharaja to ask for, and it is the obligation of the British Government to give, the aid of British troops in putting down any great popular disturbance in His Highness' territories. This arrangement affords to the Native ruler a strength and security unknown in former times. The very fact that the arrangement exists, the very knowledge that the British army will readily step in and crush the insurgents with

(i) The British army to help the Native ruler, in case of emergency.

the certainty of fate, largely prevents insurrection occurring, and British intervention puts it down.

(ii) What the exact situation is.

(ii) This is so far all very good for the ruler of a Native State, personally as a ruler. But how does it affect the people ruled? The following imaginary conversation between the people of a Native State on the one side and the British Government on the other will show the situation :—

THE BRITISH GOVERNMENT—

You, people of the Native State take note that if you rise against your ruler we shall instantly send our invincible army against you and crush you if necessary, we shall kill any number of you and capture and imprison any number. Therefore, never rise against your ruler.

THE PEOPLE—

We quite understand what you have just said, but we beg you to give us a patient hearing. Our old *mumool* was occasionally to rise against our ruler when, he, instead of preserving and promoting our welfare, cruelly oppressed us. When his oppression became unbearable, we rose against him and demanded redress. If he refused redress, we deposed him and chose another ruler who would govern us better. You now tell us that we must never rise against our ruler, and that if we do, you will shoot us down. How then, if our ruler, becoming all the more emboldened increases his oppression and tyranny? Maladministration would then proceed to any extremity and would you support it against its victims with your arms? Would it be right, would it be just, would it be acceptable to God, that you should lend your unconquerable arms to one individual oppressor to enable him to destroy the happiness and deepen the misery of hundreds of thousands of innocent fellowmen? Friends of mankind! Ardent advocates of human liberty and progress! Do you come from the distant north, only to redouble our chains and to intensify our miseries?

THE BRITISH GOVERNMENT—

By no means. Be sure that, by our wishing to support your ruler against internal disturbances, we do not at all mean that he should be enabled to misgovern you.

THE PEOPLE—

Thank you. But suppose he misgoverns as a ruler is only too apt to do when freed from the consequences of popular resentment. What then?

THE BRITISH GOVERNMENT—

In that case you may complain to us. We will certainly look into the matter. If we are satisfied that gross misgovernment is practised, we shall remonstrate with your ruler and get him to do better.

THE PEOPLE—

Quite so. But suppose he does not listen to your remonstrations and persists in gross misgovernment. How then ?

THE BRITISH GOVERNMENT—

We shall, in that case, depose him and provide a better ruler.

It would be impossible for the British Government to give other replies than those above indicated.

(iii) The ruler to govern well.

(iii) It necessarily follows, then, that the obligation of the British Government to assist the ruler of the Native State in putting down internal disorder and disturbance carries with it the right to prevent or remedy gross maladministration by that ruler. It thus becomes additionally important for the ruler to govern well and to keep the British Government satisfied that he is governing well. In connection with the subject under advertence—in order to obviate the necessity of interference by the British Government in the internal administration of the

State with the view of preventing or remedying maladministration—the great point for the Native ruler is to abstain from giving cause for his people to rise against him or to complain of gross maladministration. He cannot be too careful in this respect.

(iv) Moderate taxation and efficient police and military forces.

(iv) Let him see that taxation is moderate; make life, person and property secure, maintain a good Police backed by an efficient though small Military force; and the result will be that the great body of his people will be fairly contented and will seldom rise against him.

Some special precautions.

(5) In addition to these general conditions for the maintenance of contentment and peace, some special precautions may be here suggested.

(*a*) Religion.

(*a*) Do not interfere with the religion of the people, or any section of the people; for, religion concerns the strong feelings of large numbers.

(*b*) Taxation.

(*b*) For the same reason, do not suddenly increase any tax.

(*c*) Custom.

(*c*) For the same reason, do not suddenly change any long existing and popular custom.

(*d*) Privileges.

(*d*) Do not suddenly deprive large numbers of people of any privileges or indulgence they have long enjoyed.

(e) Restrictions.

(e) Do not suddenly impose any unusual restrictions on large numbers of people.

(f) Improvements.

(f) Do not suddenly order any such extensive Municipal improvements as would entail the destruction of a great number of houses.

(g) Discontent.

(g) Do not take any step which would suddenly spread discontent through the troops.

(h) Punishment.

(h) Even in dealing with criminal offences in which large numbers are concerned —for instance, whole villages—do not attempt to bring every one to punishment. It would often suffice to limit action to the leaders.

(i) Excitement among classes.

(i) Such classes of people as the Bheels, Waghirs, Girassias, Thakors, etc., are generally ignorant and impulsive and are known to be actuated by a common spirit. Do not give cause for a common excitement among any of these classes. In short, abstain to the utmost extent possible from all such action as is likely to cause great dissatisfaction in large numbers at the same time.

Disaffection to be rooted out.

(6) While the Native State thus pursues a just, mild and considerate policy, it should present a firm front to unprincipled and factious promoters of popular disaffection. There still are persons of this sort at

Baroda. During these six years of strong administration, they have found it necessary to be quiet. After His Highness the Maharaja assumes power at the end of the year, those persons may possibly try their old tricks. They should be closely watched. If any of them commit any mischief, they should be apprehended and brought to condign punishment in due course of law. The Maharaja's views and determination in this respect may be made sufficiently manifest in various little ways on the principle that " prevention is better than cure."

CHAPTER XLIII

Rights of the British Government

9th November, 1881.

We have now to take a view of the relations of the State with the British Government, as determined by the existing treaties and engagements. In doing this, we shall confine ourselves to the principal points, leaving minor ones to be specially studied as occasion may call for.

The relations of the State with the British Government as determined by the treaties.

(2) The State is bound to be friendly and loyal to the British Government. This is too obvious to require any detailed explanation.

The State to be loyal.

(3) The British Government should, in its turn be friendly to the State, and should do nothing against the just rights and against the welfare of the State.

The British, in turn, to be friendly.

(4) The friends and enemies of either Government shall be the friends and enemies of both. It follows that if the British Government is at war with any power, this State cannot be on

Extension of the above principle: Friends and enemies of either to be friends and enemies of both.

friendly terms with that power, but must take the side of the British Government. The principle applies also to individuals. If any individual, for instance is acting against the British Government—takes part in any political agitation or movement of any kind injurious to the British Government, —the Baroda State should not, in the least, give its support or even sympathy to such individual. Similarly, if any individual acts against the Baroda State—tries, for instance, to create disturbances in these territories—the British Government will not give its support or sympathy to such individual. On the contrary, the British Government will actually put him down. Even if the said individual live in British territory and therefore beyond the reach of the power of this State, and carry on his operations from a base in that territory the British Government will lay hold of him and bring him to punishment and adopt other preventive measures.

Abstain from use of force.

(5) This State is bound to abstain from committing any act of hostility or aggression against any power whatever. In other words, it is bound to abstain from the use of force against any State in any shape. If any differences arise between this State and any other, such differences should be referred to the British Government which will adjust the matter in a just manner in communication with His Highness'

Government. The British Government should be looked to, to enforce settlements in such matters.

(6) Accordingly, all boundary disputes—disputes about certain *giras* rights; indeed, all disputes generally between this State and any other—are brought to the notice of the British Government, who gives decisions with every desire to do impartial justice.

Boundary disputes etc. to be referred to the British Government.

(7) The Treaty provisions under advertence, applying as they do to all Native States, have put an end to those internal wars and commotions which used, formerly, to afflict all India to a deplorable degree. Peace and security have thus been insured to all States.

Peace is thus ensured.

(8) This State is bound not to entertain in its service any European or American without the consent of the British Government. The object of this provision of the Treaty is to prevent complications with European or American powers.

No European to be employed without the consent of the British.

(9) The British Government is bound to assist this State with British forces on all important occasions calling for such assistance. British Forces will accordingly be employed to protect the person of His Highness the Gaekwar, to repress and chastise rebels and exciters of disturbance in His Highness'

The British to assist the State with British forces, whenever necessary.

territories, to duly correct such subjects or dependents of His Highness, as may withhold the payment of the Sarkar's just claims, and generally to maintain tranquillity within and to prevent aggression from without.

A just Ruler will have the utmost British protection.

(10) I have, however, already explained under what necessary conditions the British Government will use its forces in the interests of the Native State. The British Government will not employ its arms to favour any injustice or oppression on the part of the Native State. This limitation should be well borne in mind. The rights accruing to the British Government, as already stated, from this obligation to render military assistance, should also be carefully carried in memory. Any oblivion in these important respects might create a false and perilous sense of security. In short, the Ruler who rules justly will have the utmost British protection.

But the State to have its own army.

(11) The treaty expressly provides that the British Subsidiary Force shall not be employed on trifling occasions. Hence it is that this State should maintain moderate and sufficiently efficient military force of its own, by means of which it may ordinarily preserve internal tranquillity without calling upon the British Government to move its battalions. It is only when an emergency occurs,

with which our own police and our own military force are not likely to be able to cope, that we can depend upon the British Government for its military assistance. Such emergencies must be rare. They must be rare in proportion as our government is good, and as our police and military forces are efficient.

What should be its strength.

(12) The Baroda State is bound to maintain a contingent of 3,000 horse for the use of the British Government. This is a very onerous obligation, and has been the source of much trouble and much discussion. This matter will, it may be expected, be placed on a more satisfactory footing in the course of time.

How tributes due to Baroda are collected.

(13) By existing arrangements with the British Government, the British Government collects the tributes (*jamabandi* and *ghasdana*) due to the Baroda State from the Princes and Chiefs and Thakors of Rewakantha, Mahikantha, Palanpur and Kathiawar, and pays over the amount to this State. And this State is bound to abstain from sending its military forces to those provinces for the collection of those dues. This arrangement, however, has not extinguished the sovereignty or the suzerainty of the Gaekwar over such of the said tribute-payers as were subject to the same at the time the said arrangement was made. The practical effect has been that the Gaekwar's rights in this respect

are exercised for His Highness by the British Political Agents of the abovementioned provinces.

Extradition of criminals.

(14) The mutual extradition of criminals is generally provided for by Treaty, and has been recently placed on a sound footing. Principles and rules have been agreed upon, which work very beneficially.

Opium and salt.

(15) Certain arrangements have also been made in these territories in relation to opium and salt. The primary object has been to aid the British Government in protecting its large revenues from its monopolies of these articles. This object has been carried out with due attention to the interests of our own subjects. It is of the utmost importance to adhere to these arrangements and to work them faithfully and vigorously.

The British guarantee to particular persons.

(16) It is to be remembered that the British Government in the early times of its relations, gave its guarantee for the right and privileges of several individuals in these territories. These guarantees became a fertile source of trouble, expense and vexation to this State, and of difficulties to the British Government itself. Fully realising this fact, the policy of the British Government has been to get rid of such guarantees as opportunities presented themselves. Accordingly, only very few such guarantees now remain. The Baroda

State should scrupulously respect these still remaining guarantees.

Guarantees to Girasias.

(17) There is another set of British guarantees which must be adverted to at this place, namely, guarantees to certain Girasias. Further particulars regarding these will be explained to His Highness by Mr. Pestonjee. I will here only suggest that the Baroda State should scrupulously respect these guarantees also.

The advice of the British Government.

(18) By treaty, His Highness the Gaekwar is bound to listen to the advice of the British Government respecting the welfare of His Highness' country. This is an important provision which has to be kept in view.

The right of the British Representative in 1828.

(19) It would also seem that the British Representative had, in 1828, the right to obtain some idea of the finances of the State, and to be consulted before any new expenses of magnitude were incurred.

The choice of the Prime Minister.

(20) The choice of his Prime Minister by His Highness the Gaekwar used to be subject to the approbation of the British Government. But in Maharaja Khande Rao's time, this condition was withdrawn, in the belief that the Gaekwar will himself exercise every care and judgment in so important a matter. The Gaekwar has thus the right to appiont his own

Minister without previously obtaining the concurrence of the British Government. The right, is a valuable one, and ought by all means to be preserved.

The Resident may be consulted in a friendly manner.

(21) Without, however, impairing that right, the Maharaja would perhaps do well, in doubtful cases, to have a little private and friendly consultation with the British Resident, in order to make sure that that authority has no serious objection to the person proposed by His Highness for the office of the Prime Minister. This course is recommended by good policy; for the complex affairs of this State can hardly be satisfactorily conducted by a Chief Minister neither deserving nor enjoying the respect of the Resident for capacity and integrity. A similar comsultation may perhaps be not undesirable when the Chief Minister is to be asked to resign. Indeed, the best method of preserving the valuable right of His Highness under advertence seems to be to take every care that any ministerial changes His Highness contemplates are not unacceptable to the British Resident.

The Viceroy's communication of 1874.

(22) As bearing on the whole subject under treatment to-day, I do well to quote here from a *Khareeta*, dated the 25th of July 1874, addressed by the Viceroy Lord Northbrook, to His Highness Mulhar Rao Gaekwar. The following extracts

from that important communication deserve special attention :—

"I deem it, therefore, necessary to remind you that both by the terms of treaties and by constant usage, the British Government has the right to advise you in public concerns affecting the good of the country, and to require the settlement, according to equity and reason, of any measures shown to be improper or unjust, and that, by consequence, it is at liberty to take such steps as it may deem necessary for the just exercise of that right, and the fulfilment of the obligations to the ruler and people of Baroda which flow therefrom.

"Your Highness must be aware that, from the earliest period of its connection with the Baroda State, the British Government has repeatedly found it necessary to intervene in Baroda affairs. This intervention has not been limited to the case of the guarantees to which Your Highness has referred but has been exercised in a variety of other ways, as for example, by investing the Resident with power of control over the finances, by assuming for a time the management of portions of the State, by the removal of evil advisers; in short, whenever intervention has been deemed by the British Government necessary in the interests of the ruler or his subjects.

"This intervention, although amply justified by the language of treaties, rests also on other foundations. Your Highness has justly observed that the British Government is undoubtedly the paramount power in India and the existence and prosperity of the Native States depend upon its fostering favour and benign protection. This is especially true of the Baroda State, both because of its geographical position intermixed with British territory, and also because a subsidiary force of British troops is maintained for the defence of the State, the protection of the person of its ruler, and the enforcement of his legitimate authority.

" My friend, I cannot consent to employ British troops to protect any one in a course of wrong-doing. Misrule on the part of a Government which is upheld by the British power is misrule in the responsibility for which the British Government becomes in a measure involved. It becomes, therefore, not only the right but the positive duty of the British Government to see that the administration of a State in such a condition is reformed and that gross abuses are removed.'

" It has never been the wish of the British Government to interfere in the details of the Baroda administration, nor is it my desire to do so now. The immediate responsibility for the Government of the States rests, and must continue to rest, upon the Gaekwar for the time being. He has been acknowledged as the Sovereign of Baroda, and he is responsible for exercising his sovereign powers with proper regard to his duties and obligations alike to the British Government and to his subjects. If these obligations be not fulfilled, if gross misgovernment be permitted, if substantial justice be not done to the subjects of the Baroda State, if life and property be not protected, or if the general welfare of the country and people be persistently neglected, the British Government will assuredly intervene in the manner which, in its judgment, may be best calculated to remove these evils and to secure good government; such timely intervention, indeed, to prevent misgovernment culminating in the ruin of the State is no less an act of friendship to the Gaekwar himself than a duty to his subjects." The Viceroy's *Khareeta* went on to say that, if the Gaekwar, to whom it was addressed, failed to attend to the advice given by the Viceroy and if, in consequence, the condition of the Baroda administration remain unreformed, that the Gaekwar would be deposed, and other arrangements would be made to secure a satisfactory administration.

The subsequent event.

(23) What followed is well known. That Gaekwar was deposed, and other arrangements were made to secure a satisfactory administration of the Baroda State. It devolves on that Gaekwar's successor to maintain such administration.

(24) The Viceroy's communication, from which I have largely quoted, deserves to be most attentively studied. The truth of it is that the British Government will not interfere in the Baroda administration so long as it is satisfactory. But if the administration becomes grossly bad, the British Government will interfere in any manner it may judge best for its reform.

The sum and substance of the communication.

(25) The right and duty of the British Government to thus exercise interference are, the Viceroy says, derived from the treaties, from constant usage, from the nature and consequences of the subsidiary alliance, and from friendship to the Gaekwar, and the duty due to his subjects.

From what the right of interference is derived.

(26) The Viceroy has indicated what constitutes bad administration. It is bad administration of justice, insecurity of life and property, persistent neglect of the general welfare of the country and people, and so forth.

What is bad administration.

(27) The Viceroy also indicates the various rights of interference on the part of the British Government. These I need not recapitulate. It is noteworthy that the removal of evil advisers from the Gaekwar is included in those rights.

Removal of evil advisers.

(28) Subsequent events—that is to say, those which followed the Viceroy's *Khareeta* —show that the rights of the British

How far the rights extend.

Government extend to the deposition of the Gaekwar himself and the substitution of another Gaekwar for the better government of the country. These rights of the British Government are extensive and are not precisely defined.

Govern well.

(29) The safest, the simplest, and the soundest way for the Maharaja to avoid or to minimise the interference of the British Government is to himself govern his country in the best manner possible.

CHAPTER XLIV

Advice of the British Government

16*th November*, 1881.

Limits to the exercise of the rights.

We have taken a survey of the rights of the British Government to interfere in Baroda affairs. Let us now consider that natural and rational limits apply to the actual exercise of those rights.

Advice to the Gaekwar.

(2) The most important of these rights is to advise His Highness the Gaekwar touching the affairs of his State. The Gaekwar is bound to listen to the advice which the British Government may give him.

The advice of the Viceroy to be distinguished from that of subordinate British Authorities.

(3) It is necessary here to draw a clear distinction between the advice of the British Government itself on the one hand, and the advice of authorities subordinate to that government on the other. The advice of the British Government is the advice of the Viceroy in Council, whereas the other advice is that of local subordinate British Authorities locally doing business. The treaty obligation to listen to advice applies to the former advice, and not to the latter. I am very far from saying that His High-

ness the Gaekwar should not listen to the latter advice. The advice coming from local subordinate British Authorities may often be very valuable and deserving of cordial acceptance by His Highness. But this advice is not that which the Gaekwar is bound by treaty to listen to. What His Highness is thus bound to listen to is the advice of the British Government itself as represented by the Viceroy and Governor-General-in-Council.

The legal difference between the two.

(4) It is manifest that the advice of the local subordinate British Authorities cannot claim to be put on the same level as the advice of the supreme British Authority in India. There is a great natural difference between the two sets of advice under comment, and the treaty makes a great legal difference between the two.

The Gaekwar not bound to accept the advice of every grade of British Authority but that of the Viceroy.

(5) By way of further explanation, I may observe that the Gaekwar would be acting contrary to the treaty if he should refuse to listen to the advice of the Viceroy, whereas His Highness could not be taxed with violation of treaty if he should for any reason, decline to accept the advice which any Political Officer, or Collector, or any other subordinate local British Authority might offer as emanating from himself. This is as it should be. If it were obligatory of the Gaekwar to accept the advice of every grade of British authority

in the same way as the advice of the Viceroy in Council, His Highness' liberty of action would be reduced to little or nothing, inasmuch as he would be obliged to accept advice coming from a plurality of sources indefinite as to its quantity, doubtful perhaps in regard to its quality, and not unfrequently conflicting in its character and its aim.

The Gaekwar is bound to listen to the advice of the Government of India.

(6) The distinction under advertence is of considerable practical importance, and deserves to be kept in view. By its being kept in view by the Gaekwar, His Highness will be free from the irritation or discontent which must result from the mistaken belief that he is obliged to accept advice coming from various sources and on any subject. On the other hand, by its being kept in view by the British Authorities who have to deal with His Highness, these authorities will be induced to be duly moderate and considerate in offering their advice, and to abstain from pressing their advice with the force which exclusively belongs to His Excellency the Viceroy in Council. The conclusion, then, is that the advice which the treaty binds His Highness the Gaekwar to listen to, is the advice of the Government of India.

How the advice may be conveyed.

(7) Such advice of the Government of India may be conveyed to the Gaekwar either directly by means of its own communications addressed to His

Highness, or indirectly through the British Resident. In the latter case, the British Resident will doubtless inform His Highness that the advice he conveys is under the Authority of the Government of India. Conveyed in either way, the advice of the Government of India will possess all the weight accorded by the treaty. When the advice is intended to carry such weight, the Government of India will, no doubt, in an express or implied manner inform His Highness that the advice is given under the treaty.

The advice should be for the good of the State.

(8) To proceed. The advice which may be given as aforesaid should, by the terms of the treaty and from natural reason, be for the good of the Baroda State; in other words, for the good of the Baroda Ruler, or of the Baroda people.

No advice opposed to the good of the State to be given.

(9) Such being the case, no advice will, it is obvious be given under the treaty, such as is opposed to the good of the Baroda State, opposed to the rights, honour and dignity of this State. For example, His Highness the Gaekwar will not be advised to recede any portion of his territories and thus to reduce his dominions. He will not be advised to surrender any part of his civil and criminal jurisdiction over his subjects. He will not be advised to lower himself from rank and position and fall to

the level of chiefs inferior to himself; and so forth.

(10) Any advice which the Government of India may give under the treaty, will, of course, be the result of due inquiry and deliberation, and as such, the advice will be for the good of this State. At any rate, the Government of India will give it under the belief that it is for the good of this State.

What is good advice.

(11) It is conceivable however, that instances may occur, though rarely, in which the Government of India indeed believes that the advice is for the good of this State, whereas His Highness the Gaekwar differs from this belief. In such instances, it is permissible for the Gaekwar to explain his own views, and endeavour to satisfy the Government of India of their correctness. In short, in doubtful cases, respectful discussion is allowable within reasonable limits. It is a priceless blessing that the British Government is pre-eminently amenable to fair and temperate reasoning. After discussion, whatever advice the Government of India may judge fit to give should, as a rule, be readily accepted under the obligation of the treaty. I say, as a rule, because there may possibly be cases in which the gravity of the question may require a reference to Her Majesty's Secretary of State

Discussion allowed in doubtful cases.

(12) Again, there must be a clear necessity for the British Government giving advice under the treaty. A necessity arising from ignorance or unwillingness on the part of the Native State in regard to the good intended to be effected by that advice. When the Native State itself is doing its work with honesty and intelligence, the best course will be to let it go on. The Government of India will, doubtless, by far prefer spontaneous progress on the part of the Native State to progress under pressure from without.

There must be a necessity for giving advice.

(13) Whenever, however, the Native State takes a decidedly and materially wrong course, it is both the right and the duty of the British Government to intervene under the treaty for the benefit of the State. It is certainly for the advantage of all the parties concerned, that maladministration should not be allowed to accumulate and reach dangerous proportions.

The British Government to intervene for the benefit of the state.

(14) In judging Native rule for purposes of giving advice under the treaty, the Government of India, will, it may be presumed, abstain from assuming too high an ideal. The standard must be that of an average well-governed Native State.

The Government of India not to place too high an ideal.

(15) It may also be presumed that the Government of India will abstain from pressing the Native State to copy British modes of administration too much. When the Native State is actuated with good intentions, it will generally be well to leave it to its own judgment how far to adopt or follow the British models. The degree of pressure to be used in regard to advice by the British Government under the treaty must, obviously, be regulated by the importance or urgency of the subject-matter of the advice. Where the object is to insure attention to the essential or fundamental conditions of ordinary good government, the British Government will be justified in using much greater pressure where, what I may call, the luxuries of good government are concerned.

The degree of pressure used in regard to advice.

(16) It may also be reasonably expected that any advice which the British Government may give under the treaty will generally be limited to large objects to be effected or to large principles to be adopted, and that the advice will not descend into details calculated needlessly to hamper the action of the Native State.

Advice not to descend into details.

(17) The manner in which the British Government will give advice under the treaty will, of course, be courteous kind and friendly, as far as may

The advice not to weaken authority.

be possible in the circumstances. At any rate, it should be as little harsh, and as little calculated to weaken the authority of the Native ruler, as may be possible.

When there is a conflict of interests, the British Government to lean to those of the people.

(18) There is one guiding principle which it may be well for His Highness the Maharaja to bear in his memory. It is a sort of key to the prevailing disposition and action of the British Government. Whenever it is possible to reconcile both, the British Government will be equally mindful of the interests of the Maharaja as a ruler, and of those of his people as his subjects. But when these two interests are materially in conflict, the British Government will generally lean to the interests of the people.

CHAPTER XLV

THE BRITISH RESIDENT

23rd November, 1881.

It is of very great importance that the relations between His Highness the Maharaja and the British Resident should be friendly and pleasant. To effect this object, attention and effort will be needed on each side.

Relations between the Maharaja and the Resident.

(2) The Maharaja should always be careful to show to the Resident every due or customary mark of respect. In these matters, His Highness should strictly follow recognised precedents. These precedents have, therefore, to be well remembered. They should be regularly recorded and occasionally consulted in order to aid His Highness' memory.

Recognised precedents to be strictly followed.

(3) When the Resident pays a visit, His Highness customarily receives him at the head of the staircase. This should be strictly adhered to, and no change should be made. Again, His Highness gives him the right side. Again, *pan supari* is given on cer-

Visits, pan-supari etc.

tain occasions. Again, *pan supari* is given according to a fixed form. All these and many other particulars should be carried out uniformly according to settled usage.

The Resident in the Dassara procession.

(4) Another instance may be here adduced just to show what minute attention is required. The Resident accompanies His Highness in the grand Dassera Procession. It is desirable to see that the elephant which the Resident rides on this occasion is of about the same height as that which His Highness rides; that the animal is made to walk fully abreast of His Highness's elephant, that the howda decorations, etc., of the animal are according to custom. Usage has settled all or most of these points and no change should be made or attempted.

All the customary respect to be shown to the Resident.

(5) In short, the Resident should have every reason to feel assured that His Highness is, at all times, most anxious to show him all the respect due and customary. The Resident should not have the slightest reason to suspect that His Highness would wish to diminish those marks of respect, if any opportunity offered for doing so. An example may be useful to explain what is meant. Suppose that, on any occasion the Resident is, by custom, entitled to sit on the right side of His Highness, but that from ignorance or inadvertence, the Resident

takes the left side. In such a case, His Highness should not take advantage of the mistake of the Resident but he should at once offer to the Resident the right side.

Regret any error.

(6) If, in spite of every care and attention, any mark of respect due to the Resident happens to be omitted on any occasion, His Highness should take the earliest opportunity to express his regret for the accident.

The Resident's attitude towards the Maharaja.

(7) Such feelings and action on the part of His Highness may well be expected to be cordially and constantly reciprocated by the British Resident. The British Resident should invariably accord to His Highness all the respect due to His Highness in conformity with custom, and in recognition of His Highness' position as the sovereign of the country. His Highness should have every reason to feel assured that the Resident is, at all times, most anxious to do His Highness all the honour to which His Highness is entitled. His Highness should not have the slightest reason to suspect that the Resident would wish to diminish any marks of respect if an opportunity offered for doing so. Briefly, then each of the high personages concerned should fully and cordially give and take whatever is due. They should have no jealousies, no fears, no suspicions in this respect. Then the intercourse between them will be quite smooth and friendly.

(8) Do not attempt to make any presents to the Resident beyond the customary ones of flowers and fruit, and such trifles. British officers are strictly prohibited from receiving any presents of value; and they are generally too conscientious to secretly evade such prohibition. In short, do not ever even appear desirous of laying any British officer under obligation to you in any undue or underhand manner.

No presents to the Resident.

(9) If any information or papers be wanted from the Residency, apply direct to the Resident himself. Never attempt to obtain any, surreptitiously.

Apply to the Resident for any information.

(10) Everything that may be spoken or written to the Resident, whether officially or otherwise must be scrupulously correct in point of facts. Veracity of the highest order should mark the same. Any default in this respect would soon be fatal to confidence and esteem. Courtesy and perfect good temper also should mark everything that may be spoken or written to the Resident. This applies both to matter and manner. Courtesy and good temper are necessary when a difference of opinion is to be expressed or discussed.

Communications to the Resident, verbal or written.

(11) Some differences of opinion will occasionally arise. But these should be reduced to the smallest possible number. In a large proportion of instances

Judicious compromise, where there is difference of opinion.

inquiry, consultation and calm reflection will dissipate the grounds of difference and bring about an agreement. In other instances, judicious compromises should be effected. In others again, where the interests involved are trifling or transitory, the one party may yield in deference to the other.

When official discussion is necessary.

(12) There will thus remain a few instances in which the interests at stake are important and the difference of views is considerable. Such instances will necessitate official discussion. In such instances the communication representing His Highness' views should be very carefully drawn up, so that, when they go up to the higher authorities of the British Government, they may produce the desired effect. Those communications should be, so far as possible, complete and comprehensive in themselves, in language and tone, they should be courteous and respectful; in facts and arguments, they should be perfecty correct and clear, and the principles therein appealed to should be those which are well recognised by the British Government.

Experienced administrative officers to draw up communications.

(13) I would avail myself of this opportunity to suggest that lawyers, howsoever able, are not the best fitted to draw such communications, unless they are practised in political correspondence also. The

style in which a lawyer may address a judge and that in which a Maharaja should address the British Government are in some respects materially different. The lawyer's arguments may always be utilized, but the Maharaja's communications should be drawn up by experienced administrative officers. I may add that similar remarks are applicable to editors of newspapers, whether natives or Europeans.

The Resident to send the Maharaja's communications in their integrity to the higher authorities.

(14) In referring any differences of opinion to the higher authorities, it is only right and proper that the Resident should send up in their integrity the communications which convey the Maharaja's views and arguments. It would hardly be fair to send up only extracts or summaries, for the Maharaja should not be deprived of the satisfaction of feeling that he has been fully heard.

The Maharaja's rights to be properly defended.

(15) With every necessary care and caution, the referring of a difference of opinion to higher authorities may sometimes involve a certain amount of unpleasantness. But obviously, this should not deter the Maharaja from requesting or allowing such a reference where his rights, honour and dignity or the welfare of his subjects is concerned. These need always to be defended with firmness as well as with wisdom and moderation. To

defend these properly is the imperative duty of the Maharaja. If they be not vigilantly and vigourously defended, they would gradually decline and might eventually disappear. The British Government cannot blame a Maharaja for thus defending interests which Her Majesty's great Proclamation of 1858 has declared to be as inviolable as if they were Her Majesty's own.

The double capacity of the British Resident.

(16) When the Maharaja's views and wishes in these respects commend themselves to the Resident's sense of justice, the Resident may be fairly expected to give his full and cordial support to them in his communications to superior authorities. In this connection, it is to be remembered that the British Resident has practically a double capacity. He is the protector of British interests, but he is also the protector of the interests of the Native State. It might perhaps, have been otherwise if the Native State had its own representative of its interests at the court of His Excellency the Viceroy. But such is not the case. As matters stand, the Resident has to represent the interests of the British Government to the Maharaja and has also to represent the interests of the Maharaja to the British Government. Such a situation requires that the British Resident should hold the balance even between the two sides, that he should exercise perfect impartiality. It follows that he should not shrink from

the duty of justly protecting the interests of the Native State when occasion demands it. It has been my good fortune to see not a few British Residents conscientiously high-minded enough to perform this duty even at the risk of temporary displeasure on the part of their superiors. It is this high order of political morality, it is this elevated standard of public duty which constitutes one of the main sources of strength and durability to the British Empire.

The Resident's ideal of duty.

(17) The fact, really, is that a Native State practically sees little of the character and quality of the British Government, except through the British Resident. As the British Resident appears to it, so it supposes the British Government to be. All the just and general assurances of Her Majesty, all the beneficent and magnanimous avowals of the Viceroy have little practical value to the Native State except as given effect to by the local British Representative. The British Resident has, therefore, to represent fully and faithfully all the disinterestedness, the justice, the moderation, the generosity and the friendly spirit which are the attributes of the British Government itself. The Agent's ideal of duty should be quite as high as that of the Principal. The Resident should be relied upon also to protect the State against any aggressive tendencies on the part of neigh-

bouring Political Agents and other British officers.

Maintain principles already established.

(18) The Maharaja should firmly maintain and cling to the various solutions of important or difficult questions which have been made during His Highness' minority. They are the results of very elaborate consideration on the part of the several authorities concerned. They have got rid of many sources of confusion and controversy. They have established or restored right principles. His Highness should therefore strictly enjoin his officers to keep those settlements in view and not to depart from them at all. If in any instance the Residency loses sight of them, His Highness' officers should invariably refer the Residency to them.

Consult the Resident freely.

(19) In all important matters, His Highness will, no doubt, have sound views submitted to him by his council. If, however, His Highness should still feel any great doubt or difficulty, His Highness may freely consult the Resident, who will give disinterested advice. Some matters may be so important that, even without feeling any doubt or difficulty, His Highness will do well to talk them over with the Resident in order to secure the benefit of that authority's concurrence and sympathy. On the other hand, too frequently troubling the Resident might imply some deficiency of thinking and

governing capacity in the Native State. Consultation with the Resident may well be made by His Highness' instructions. In special cases requiring such a course, His Highness may himself consult the Resident personally.

Let the Dewan offer his own views.

(20) Important matters should not, I submit, be settled off hand and orally between His Highness and the Resident, without giving an opportunity to His Highness' Dewan to supply information to afford explanations, and to offer his own views in the interests of the State.

What is orally settled to be reduced to writing.

(21) If any thing be orally settled, it should by no means be left in that state. Better reduce the thing to writing; otherwise great vagueness and uncertainty and probably misapprehensions and unpleasantness might ensue. As a rule, no important matter should be considered settled until the settlement is inscribed on paper and communicated in this form.

The Resident to inform the Maharaja, before sending any proposal to the British Government

(22) There should be an understanding that, wherever possible, the Resident should not send up to the British Government any proposal affecting His Highness' interests without previously ascertaining His Highness' views. This is a right principle, and it would obviate the Resident committing himself, under imperfect information, to any proposal and

feeling the embarrassments necessarily arising therefrom.

The Resident not to interfere in the Maharaja' exercise of patronage.

(23) So long as His Highness carefully selects men for appointments and promotions, the Resident may be expected to abstain from all interference in the exercise of patronage, interference, direct or indirect, official, demi-official; and private experience has shown beyond all doubt, that, where the Native Government is good, such abstinence is extremely necessary for its efficiency.

Replies to the Resident to be promptly despatched.

(24) His Highness should see that replies are sent to the Resident's references as promptly as may be possible, though, of course, hasty replies are to be avoided where the matter is of importance in itself or as involving an important principle.

The Maharaja to correspond only through the Resident.

(25) It is a strict rule that His Highness cannot write on any matter of business to the higher authorities of the British Government, independently of the British Resident. Every business communication from His Highness must be either addressed to the Resident or addressed to the higher authorities through the Resident. The rule is so strict that I would advise His Highness to adhere to it, even in regard to letters of ordinary courtsey or compliment.

Do not trust to the efficiency of 'khatpat'.

(26) I would earnestly advise His Highness not to trust to the efficiency of *khatpat*. Persons are still to be found who may come and whisper that they have great personal influence with the Viceroy or the Governor, or with his councillors and that they are willing to use that influence in His Highness' favour. They may even venture to pretend to similar influence over the authorities in England. Such persons are generally unprincipled and wish to obtain money under false pretences. They must not be countenanced. They must be firmly avoided as they are sure not only to take away money but to bring discredit on His Highness.

Payments to the Residency Treasury.

(27) The State has to make several payments to the Residency Treasury on various accounts. Such payments should be made, whenever they become due, without any delay.

Help to be given to the Assistant Resident.

(28) On the part of the State, cordial assistance should be given to the Assistant Resident who is in charge of the Thuggi and Dacoity Departments. Properly worked, this department does much good in pursuing Thugs and Dacoits wherever they may go. At the same time, some vigilance may be desirable in view to prevent the detectives of the department oppressing innocent people, and to

prevent the department itself unconsciously encroaching on the rights of the State.

The rights of the Resident and members of his staff to be duly respected.

(29) There are certain special rights and privileges enjoyed by the British Resident and also by the members of his staff and even by servants, so also by the British troops stationed here. The State and its officers should be careful not to interfere with those rights and privileges. In short, duly honour the British Representative, cultivate friendly relations with him, and win his confidence and support by a steady straight-forward policy based on the best principles of government.

CHAPTER XLVI

Conclusion

1st *December*, 1881.

Concluding advice.

As we are now very near the epoch when Your Highness will assume the government of your country, I must bring these lectures to a close. Had time allowed, I should have gone on for some months more. Yet what my esteemed colleagues and myself have so far communicated to Your Highness may suffice, I trust, to indicate the great principles which a good ruler has faithfully to adhere to, in order to make his subjects contented and prosperous and thereby himself acquire honour and distinction.

The position of a Maharaja.

(2) Your Highness has now a fair idea of the great responsibilities which are inseparable from great power. The position of a Maharaja in these days is not one of abundant ease and unlimited enjoyment, it is not one in which he is at liberty to spend what public

money he likes and in what manner he pleases, it is not one in which power can be exercised without salutary constitutional restraint, it is not one in which the will of His Highness is the law. In these days a fierce light beats on the throne. It is a light which exposes every defect to the public gaze. It is a light which has immensely increased the responsibilities of rulers.

His great responsibilities.

(3) The Maharaja is responsible in various directions in regard to all his actions. He is responsible to God, and to his own conscience. He is responsible to established principles. He is responsible to his people. He is responsible to the British Government. He is responsible to enlightened public opinion in general.

Adhere faithfully to good principles.

(4) The principles with which Your Highness has become acquainted will largely enable you to discharge these responsibilities satisfactorily; Your Highness will remember those principles, Your Highness will allow others to remind you of those principles. Knowing and remembering good principles is not, however, the most difficult part of the duty of a ruler. The most difficult and the most important part is to adhere constantly and faithfully to those principles. This involves great self-denial. It requires great firmness in resisting multifarious seductive influences.

High ideal of duty.

(5) Your Highness will have always to maintain a high ideal of duty. This requires that you should surround yourself with advisers who have such an ideal of duty.

Under God's blessing, may Your Highness' career be long, happy and honourable, and pre-eminently distinguished for justice, wisdom and benevolence.

INDEX.

Index.